In this exciting new book Helen Parrott takes a walk through the seasons, offering a practical guide on how to get in touch with the natural world through the passing seasons to create distinctive works of textile art. Based upon the view that we all benefit from feeling connected to and grounded in the world around us, *Mark-Making Through the Seasons* is filled with projects and step-by-step technique guides to inspire textile students and professionals alike.

Helen Parrott explains how mark-making techniques can be used meditatively to record our surroundings and events in our lives, and how they are influenced by seasonal changes of colour, energy and light. She encourages you to connect to your own locality, to explore the creative potential of what is around you – whether urban or rural, at home or on holiday – and use specific seasonal aspects to create a personal, working cycle of textile art.

From learning how to spot the first signs of Spring to recording seasonal characteristics – equinox through to solstice – this book teaches you how to experience and explore the passing seasons for inspiration. A wealth of practical techniques and projects are scattered throughout and Helen guides you through every stage of the creative process, teaching the basics of both hand and machine stitch techniques, working with free-form stitching, chain stitch and corded quilting as well as appliqué, collage and running stitch. Helen also shows how to work with dot and line, repeating patterns, light and shadow, colour, and plant structures. The book explores how walking throughout the year can bring inspiration and encourage time for reflection; making and collating samples; observing new places and cultures; finding creative inspiration in the history of the place and reviewing and displaying finished textile artworks.

Mark-making reminds us that wherever we may live, there is unbound beauty in the subtle and the bold seasonal fluctuations. This creative guide helps you become familiar with and inspired by the changing natural world to create thoughtful works of textile art.

Mark-Making
Through the Seasons

BATSFORD

HELEN PARROTT

Mark-Making
Through the Seasons

TEXTILE ART INSPIRATION AND TECHNIQUES

Dedication

For M – our shared love of landscape
has taken us a long way so far.

First published in the United Kingdom
in 2019 by

Batsford
43 Great Ormond Street
London
WC1N 3HZ

An imprint of
Pavilion Books Company Ltd

ISBN 9781849945790

A CIP catalogue for this book is
available from the British Library.

10 9 8 7 6 5 4 3 2 1

Reproduction by Mission Productions,
Hong Kong
Printed and bound by Toppan Leefung
Printing Ltd, China

This book can be ordered direct from
the publisher at
www.pavilionbooks.com,
or try your local bookshop.

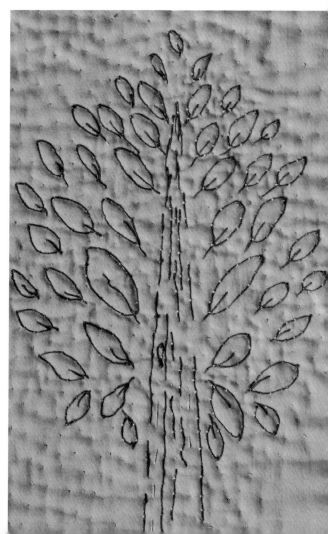

Contents

Introduction

Whether you are new to making textiles and textile art or more experienced, welcome to this book. Creating is a fundamental human activity and we are fortunate that for many of us the making of stitched textiles provides joy and pleasure. Through this book I hope to encourage and support you to explore and build on that joy and pleasure through sharing the ideas, techniques and examples that have worked for me as I have deepened my own creative life and practice over the years.

Working with a seasonal focus in my life and my textile-making has deepened my engagement with, and my enjoyment and pleasure in both. I seek to encourage you to experiment and develop your own experience of and ideas about the passing seasons, and to use this knowledge to make personal and distinctive textile work, reflecting the seasons in your own surroundings and life.

In an increasingly fast-moving, urbanizing and changing world where most people live in cities, we may think that the seasons of the natural world are somehow less relevant and important to us. This book is based on my strongly held view that we all benefit from feeling connected to and grounded in the world around us. Observing and drawing inspiration from the changing seasons around us to make distinctive and personal textile art can enhance this connection.

Greater awareness and appreciation of our seasonal surroundings can often calm and centre us. There is beauty and joy in noticing both the subtle and the bold seasonal events going on around us. Appreciating the momentary transience of a rainbow, the visual effects of a heavy storm or feeling the drama of the arrival of spring over several weeks can help us focus and be present. Wherever we may live, there are distinctive seasonal or daily aspects of light and shade, colour and form to observe, explore, become familiar with and be inspired by.

Handmade marks in concrete lit by early spring sunlight

Summer poppies at
Filey, North Yorkshire

This book is focused on the annual cycle of the passing seasons
and approaches textile art from a different standpoint than my first
book *Mark Making in Textile Art* (Batsford, 2013). The content of this
book reflects my evolving thinking and new teaching, experiences
and ideas since then; hence the two books are complementary,
but can also stand alone.

This book draws on my own practice as a textile artist, teacher
and writer over many years. It is a book of starting points, ideas
and suggested ways to engage with your local surroundings and
your own creativity. It is definitely not intended as a blueprint for
you to copy. You have your own unique creative life to live, locality
to explore and personal art to make. My aim is to encourage and
support you to find some of that uniqueness and then to apply it
creatively through the medium of textiles. I hope that seeing my
examples, works-in-progress and finished works will prompt you
to explore your own surroundings and life for inspiration.

Structure of this book

In my locality, the seasons do not occur as four distinct time periods, each with clear start and end dates. It is all so much more subtle and beautiful than that. Each successive day can bring very different inspiration, yet when I stand back the broad seasons are clear. The exact months of each season will differ from place to place around the world. The ideas here are intended to inspire you and to be adapted to suit your individual location. I have used the generic names of the seasons here – spring, summer, autumn and winter – referring only to specific months or dates where there is a festival or event of particular note, such as the solstices and equinoxes.

I have chosen to structure the content of the book around four seasonal chapters, beginning with spring. Each seasonal chapter is subdivided based on what I consider to be key creative aspects during that season. The many glories and subtleties of spring merited a chapter with four seasonal subsections, while the Summer, Autumn and Winter chapters have two subsections each.

The ten seasonal aspects I have chosen to focus on, under the main headings, are:

Spring
First signs
First colours
Equinox: light and dark
Expanding colour

Summer
Midsummer
Harvest

Autumn
Autumn colour
Structures and processes

Winter
Sound and light
Winter wet
Winter cold

These are just ten of the many possibilities I considered and 'auditioned' for inclusion. There is so much material that I could have included, potentially enough for another book. My final choices are intended to offer a balance of images, ideas, approaches and techniques across the book as a whole.

Each seasonal subsection begins with an observational walk, followed by exploratory paper- and stitch-based exercises. These explorations are invitations to explore images, ways of working, marks and stitch, or combinations of all these. This book is illustrated throughout with photographs from my seasonal walks, exploratory paperworks, developmental samples and completed textile artworks.

This introduction and the four seasonal chapters are followed by Chapter 5 covering the following topics: ways of working including making samples; being inspired while away from home; being inspired by history and archives; reviewing your textile work annually; and finishing work. Holidays are important and enjoyable activities for many of us, offering time for rest and renewal, inspiration and reflection as well as opportunities to explore and experience new and inspiring places. When coming home after time away or a holiday, I returned to my local walks. To my surprise, I saw these familiar places anew, sometimes sharply so. I began to understand that time away and holidays offer useful insights to support creative work.

Chapter 6 covers equipment and materials, followed by a resources section with books, websites and supplier information. Finally there is a section that gives background to the writing of this book for those who would like to know more of the story of its genesis.

Landscape of thawing snow seen from Stanage Edge

How to use this book

Not all of the content in this book will feel relevant and useful to you now. So I encourage you to work through the book once over the course of a year or two, and then revisit it, dipping into the text at whatever point in the year you may find yourself. It may be that the ideas and suggestions for winter, for example, benefit from your fuller experience and observation of more than one winter in your locality.

Making stitched textiles

Creative activities, such as making stitched textiles, where you choose the pace, make the decisions and can lose yourself in the process for a few hours can be a solace and a source of comfort and strength in difficult times. Stitching, particularly when done by hand, can provide a space of calm amidst the bustle of day-to-day living and routine tasks. Making textiles can also offer opportunities to travel, to learn and share skills, to meet with like-minded people and to develop a greater awareness of place, people and history. We may make quilts or clothes for loved ones, or smaller stitched pieces for our homes and sometimes for an exhibition. Initially we may make textiles only for our personal and family use, while later we may find and develop an individual artistic approach to stitch. Over time we may develop our own distinctive creative voice, sometimes leading to exhibiting in a fine-art context. All of these activities and more make up the broad, exciting and life-enhancing world of contemporary textiles.

Studio

In this book I use the term 'studio' to mean wherever you make your textile work. A dedicated room to make textile work is a nice thing to have, but it is not essential. For me, making sometimes takes place in my studio at home, often in a hotel room or on a train, sometimes in the garden or kitchen. What matters is to be creative and make distinctive personal textile artwork; where you work is less important.

Ways of working with the seasons

Thinking and working on a seasonal basis is nothing new, of course. Agriculture, industry, religion and education all have their different seasonal rhythms and influences across the world. Historic dates and seasonal festivals still structure and influence our lives.

There are many ways in which the seasons can influence your work and creative life. When you pause to consider it, you may notice that the changing seasons already influence when you do specific activities. You may make less textile work in the summer than in the winter for example. The lure of the long summer days will take you outside to the hills or coast, the garden or the allotment and your making time may reduce accordingly. When the longer nights of autumn and winter return, staying in at home, making and thinking, may be more attractive.

The seasons can inspire and influence your textile work in many ways: visually, through all your senses, through the mood and energy of the season you find yourself experiencing. Examples of these approaches are shared throughout the book.

1. What you see
'What you see' are the visual representations of the season. For example, a view, detail or colour can be used fairly directly to inspire textile work. The photograph opposite of autumn cherry-tree leaves, showing many shades of pink, apricot, yellow and green, could easily be adapted to provide a harmonious colour scheme for a textile piece.

The photograph of scored crossed marks at the start of this chapter could easily be adapted for a boldly cross-stitched textile. This photograph was taken in the morning of an early spring day when the low angle of the sunlight made the marks really stand out. At another season, with different lighting, these strong handmade marks might not have caught my eye at all.

2. What you experience

Each season has its own distinctive sensory aspects affecting all five senses. This book concentrates on the visual, but noticing and appreciating the seasonal sounds, textures, tastes and scents as well can add much enjoyment to your experiences. The smell of the earth after spring rain or the dry rustle of a single autumn leaf blowing down the road can provide small moments of pleasure.

Cherry leaves in autumn

3. Mood and energy

Consider, too, the emotions and feelings you experience while you are out walking and observing at different seasons. What is the mood, energy and feeling of that time of day, experienced at that time of year? How could that mood and energy experience inspire and influence your textile work? The photograph shown on page 15 was taken in winter, towards sunset. It has a quiet, pale mood, which could inspire a choice of colours (pale and muted), techniques (hand stitch) and materials (soft fabrics made of natural fibres). The result could be a quilt that is soft to handle, subtly hand stitched in pale grey/mauve, apricot, white and pale, peachy pink. A pale and unevenly dyed fabric, perhaps rejected for other projects as too wishy-washy, could be perfect here.

4. Blending and integrating

Blending and integrating some, or all, of these approaches to the seasons can help you develop and create personally satisfying textiles. My examples include the *Radiant* pieces shown in the Spring chapter (see page 45) and the *Comfort Blanket* quilt illustrated at the end of the Winter chapter (see page 99).

Seasons, places and people

The seasons are experienced by us in real time among the places and landscapes where we live. The many interactions of people with those places over time has strongly influenced what we see and experience today. Our interactions may be transient – the long shadow of a person in evening sunlight leaves no lasting mark. A photograph may be the only record of such a moment. By way of contrast, the walls and enclosures made by generations of people in local landscapes can date back many hundreds, indeed thousands, of years. Place is a fundamental part of experiencing and working creatively with the seasons. Your own place will offer unique aspects and opportunities for creative inspiration.

At first sight my interest appears to be in the natural world around me, especially plants and trees. Of course, a truly 'natural' landscape is a rarity in Britain and many other parts of the world. Many of the apparently 'natural' inspirational seasonal experiences included here are actually the outcome of human activity over varying periods of time. Plants and trees are the visible outcomes of the ways people have used, owned and managed the land in my locality for millennia. The local moorlands covered in purple heather in the late summer are a well-known and wonderful sight. They are actually the result of managed grazing on the moorland for shooting. Similarly the beauty of bluebell woods and hay meadows are the visible outcomes of specific land-management practices.

You may find it interesting and worthwhile to think about and make some notes of the seasonal and longer term tracks and traces of human activities you can see in your locality. On page 126 is a list of tracks and traces of human activity in my locality to encourage you to explore this aspect of where you live. My list is not exhaustive and yet it contains enough starting points for a lifetime of creative work.

Spring comes earlier where there is shelter and warmth. Flowers bloom earlier in sunny garden borders or on roadsides than on north-facing hill slopes. In my own locality spring appears first in the small patches of snowdrops at the base of garden walls. Gradually these patches grow, joining up into larger and larger areas. Observing these tiny, very local microclimates is important

in understanding the distinctive effects of the seasons in your locality. Winter sunset
Think of the Japanese custom of celebrating spring when the cherry
blossom comes into flower, first in the south and then moving gradually
north across the country. I encourage you to observe such seasonal
timings in your own locality.

Walking

Each section of the book includes a walk, sometimes two, to encourage
you to understand and become familiar with your own locality in each
season of the year. These walks can be short strolls round the garden or
local park, a visit to the allotment or longer walks – whatever suits your
location, energy and physical abilities. The key thing is that the walks
are easy for you to reach because access facilitates the development of
familiarity. In practice, this usually means walking close to home. Patient
observation and experience over years will also enable you to tailor your
walks to make the most inspirational use of the weather, time of day and
time of year.

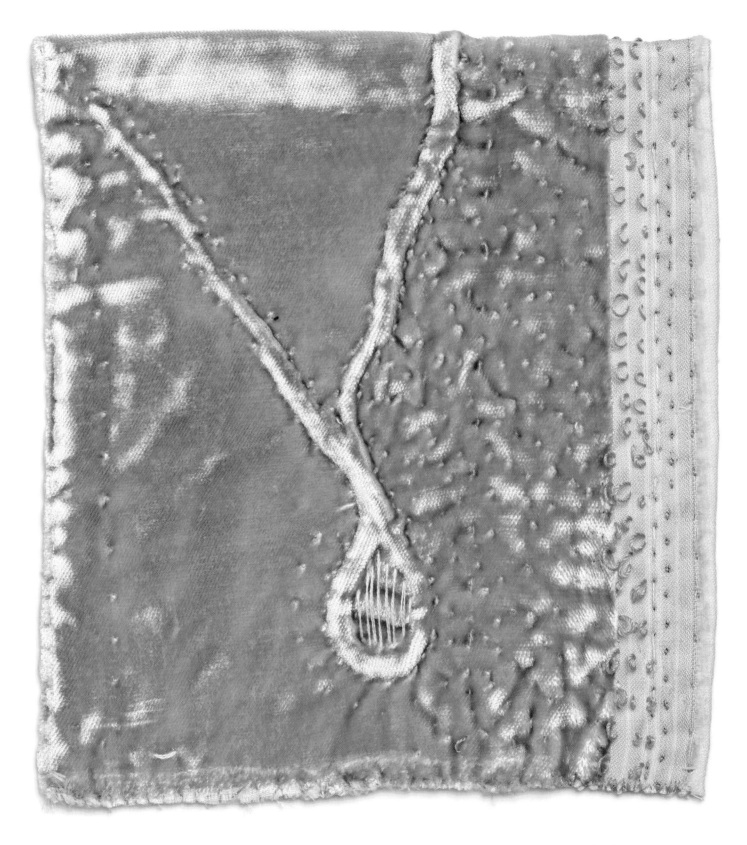

Candlemas sample:
hand stitches and
cording on velvet

Walks, whether taken alone or in company, offer time out, an opportunity to use all your senses more fully and appreciate the wonder of the world around you. Walking can also help to clear and focus the mind, provide time to mull over and make creative decisions and lift the spirit. Each season has its specific colours, textures, smells, sounds and sights, which can often inspire creativity in textiles and stitch. I usually take my mobile phone or digital camera on my walks, taking many photographs on my way. I seek to capture moments or glimpses of things that appeal to me. My aim is not technical excellence: I seek to record through photography and occasional notes and sketches whatever appeals to me so I can reconnect with it in the future.

Many of the illustrations in this book came from walks near my home and appear to be mostly rural because I now live on the edge of a big city. While a rural locality may appear to be more creatively inspiring than an urban one, don't be put off walking and using this book if you live within a city. Gardens (whether your own or other people's) and parks can provide rich resources of creative inspiration. Street trees are an obvious connection to the natural world, especially deciduous trees such as planes, horse chestnuts or acers. Beauty is to be found in some surprising urban places and the tiny details of seasonal life in a city can be as inspiring and intriguing as those seen in the deepest rural areas.

Safety

In both urban and rural contexts you need to walk safely and responsibly with an awareness of hazards, although the nature of the particular hazard will depend on the location and weather, of course. Groups of curious cattle are not usually found in city streets, for example. I do often walk alone, but only where I feel safe to do so and when others know where I am and when I will be back.

Explore and experience

My aim in sharing this seasonal way of thinking and making with you is to encourage you to explore and experience the opportunities for inspiration in your own locality. I encourage you to work with your experience of the colours, forms, moods and energies of the seasons around you to create stitched textile work that is deeply personal and resonant for you. Let us begin with the gentle subtleties of early spring.

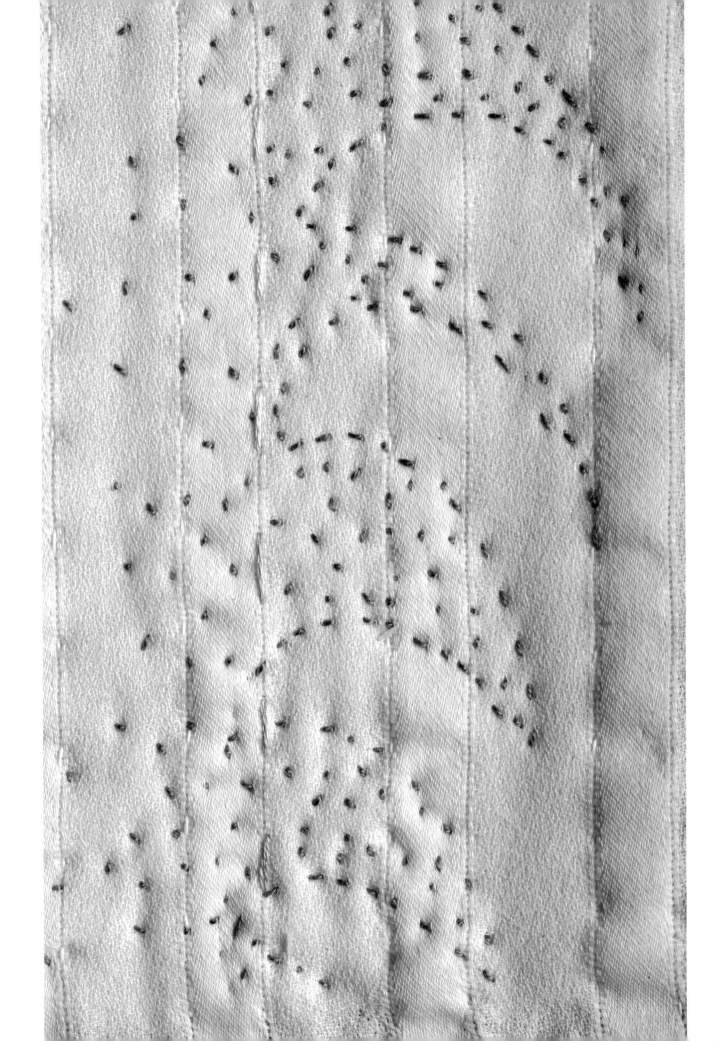

CHAPTER 1

Spring

Spring is the ideal place to begin working with the seasons. The arrival of spring usually encourages a sense of new energy and expanding opportunities. This sense of new beginnings sits well with a book aimed at exploring new sights and ideas for textile work.

This Spring chapter has four subsections, reflecting the wide range of inspiration at this time of year. These are: First signs; First colours; Equinox light and dark; Expanding colour.

Detail of Tree of Life
sample stitched with
dots and dashes

First signs

Very early in February is usually when the first signs of spring appear where I live. Here, on the southern edge of the Pennines, these very first stirrings are fleeting, tentative and delicate. The daylight becomes a touch less hard and grey, with moments of an exquisite pale yellow light, and it lasts a little longer each day. Sometimes there is strong sunshine and real warmth once again. These tiny changes, lasting only moments, a few hours at most, can be visible one day and gone the next. Noticing these micro-changes lifts my spirit, and inspires and renews me creatively after the stillness, wet and cold of winter.

Less known than the Christian festivals of Christmas and Easter is the festival of Candlemas on 2 February. Candlemas seems an apt name for this time of gentle, flickering daylight. Creatively and visually this is a time of soft, warming energy, of the palest of yellows, whites, creams and yellow greens. The photograph here of low, slanting sunlight passing between tree trunks and falling onto the woodland floor captures the beginning of spring for me. It is time to get out into the world around you; into the woods, the fields, the park and perhaps onto the moors and hills.

Slanting low sunlight
between tree trunks

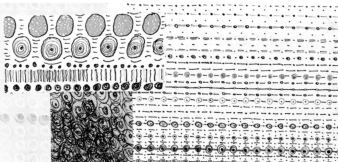

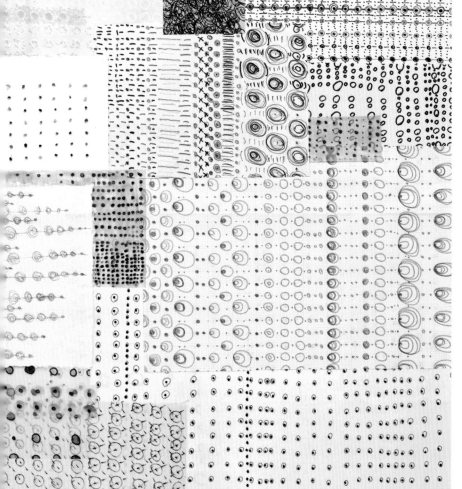

First signs walk

At the very first hint of spring in your locality, however fleeting, find time to go for a local walk, taking your camera with you. Observe the world around you as it is starting to change. Inhale, go slowly, travel hopefully, savouring your surroundings, noticing and enjoying any warmth from the sun, seeing how the light falls and where the shadows are. Notice, for example, that walking through woodland smells different to walking in fields.

Find places where seeds and plants are beginning to grow. Keep looking for the tiny shapes and dots of new life. Maybe there are carpets of snowdrops or yellow aconites somewhere locally. What is the first growth where you live? Take lots of close-up photographs of what you see, especially details of things you may have never looked at closely before. What surprises you?

Exploring first signs

Back home, review your photographs, selecting one or two with interesting dots or tiny marks to develop further. Assemble a range of different types and sizes of subtly coloured papers (cream, pale yellow, off white, palest greens and so on). Tracing, tissue and watercolour papers are good options. Gather a range of coloured felt-tipped and other pens and inks.

Find a space to work and begin by making dots and tiny marks on the various papers you have gathered, using all the pens you have. Work with bigger and smaller dots and marks, even and uneven, hollow or solid dots, grouped or kept separate or spread randomly. Make some of your dots and marks in lines; try making marks in slanting lines echoing the low angle of early spring daylight. Then try making grids of dots of different sizes. Keep working until you either run out of time, or of inspiration.

Look at all your drawings and interesting marks from the previous exercise. Then repeat the mark-making process using coloured fabric pens or crayons on pale fabrics. Dress or quilting-weight cotton fabric is a good choice. The subtle and irregular colours of space-dyed fabrics and threads work well to reflect the tentative and irregular appearance of the first signs of spring growth. Use masking tape to attach the fabric pieces to a flat surface to keep them smooth as you draw.

Above: Buds and other signs of first growth

Far left: Dot drawings

Exploring first signs in hand stitch

Now let's begin to explore this gentle mood through hand stitch. Find some small pieces of pale, soft, washed or worn natural fabrics (calico, felt, linen, cotton). Choose two fabrics of the same weight to work with – one could come from the fabrics you created earlier with drawn marks. The top layer should be the most visually interesting fabric. Add a middle layer of lightweight wadding. Cut each piece into a square of around 20cm (8in).

Assemble a selection (six to ten types) of cotton, linen and silk threads suitable for hand stitching. These can be machine sewing threads, as well as specialist hand-embroidery threads. Ideally your choice of threads will include subtle and slightly sheeny ones to echo the sense of gentleness at this time of year.

Inspired by your earlier drawings, using a washable marker pen, draw dots and dashes randomly, in slanting lines, or in grids onto your chosen top fabric to provide some guidance for placing your stitches. Then sandwich your three layers together, pinning or tacking them as needed to hold them securely. Then hand stitch along your guide marks in running stitch, removing the pins/tacking as you go along. Notice how the small stitches pull down into the wadding and the fabric around them is raised.

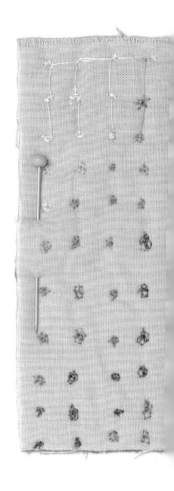

Above right: Sample showing a variety of machine-sewn dots

Above: Germinating crops

Going further: machine stitch

For contrast, experiment with a machine stitch on three layers of fabric, creating free-machined dots of varying sizes placed randomly, in lines or grids. A washable marker pen may be useful here to provide some guide marks for your machine stitching.

The samples shown provide some starting points. The sample at the top is stitched on space-dyed vintage fabric and the dark green sample below it is the reverse side of the same sample, showing the difference the choice of background fabric makes. Sometimes the connecting threads have been removed to separate the dots; others have been left uncut, creating a different effect.

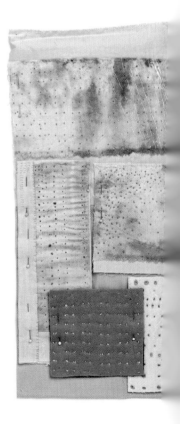

Going further: adding loops

After you have explored the potential of dots on paper and fabric sufficiently, choose one or two of your dotted fabrics to explore further through hand stitch by adding small loops akin to the shapes of germinating crops. The loops are created by not quite pulling the thread all the way through when making each stitch. The size of the loop can be varied by altering the amount of thread left on the surface each time. The thread can be knotted on the reverse after each stitch to ensure the loops do not move. If you

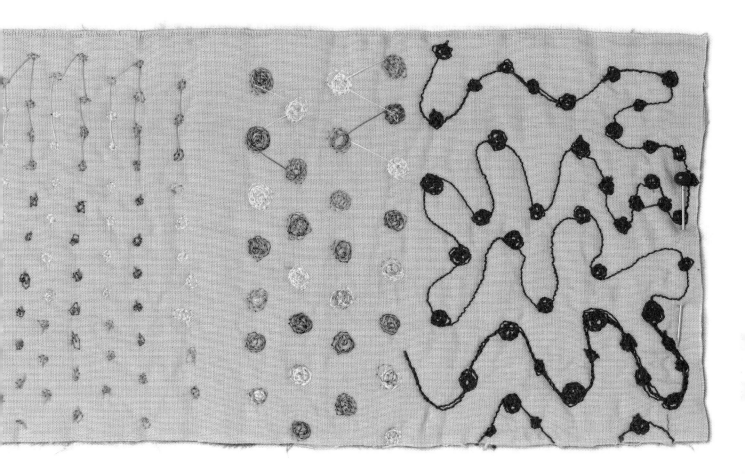

prefer, the sample can be finished by ironing a layer of Bondaweb and fabric on the reverse side to secure the stitches in position.

For the samples overleaf I used the idea of slanting light to inspire the drawing of my sloping guidelines. For the lower sample, iron-on smocking dots were applied to the cream calico top layer to provide a guide for the stitching. The grid of loops and dots worked in green cotton perle and white linen threads is incomplete, exploring the idea of partially germinated seeds in flowerbeds and fields. Some of the larger loops are knotted on the surface to add extra visual interest.

More development of these ideas and samples could lead to a series of textile pieces based on the stages of seed germination and growth.

Left: Group of hand-sewn dot and long slanting stitch samples

Right: Reverse of sample above, showing connecting threads still attached

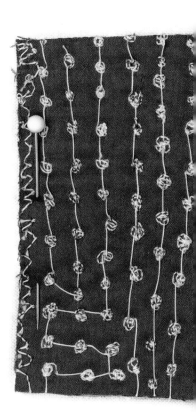

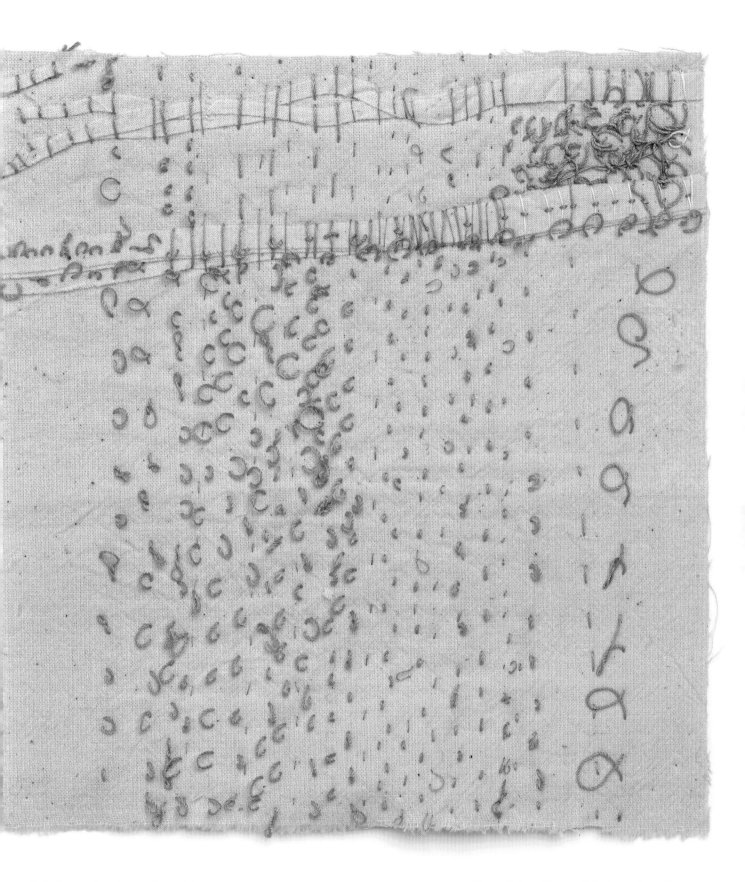

Left: Group of hand-sewn dot-and-loop stitch samples

Above: Dots and loops stitched on calico with green silk thread with a slight sheen, evoking the gloss seen on some new plant growth

First colours

As well as the greens usually associated with spring, there are other colours to be seen by the observant person, so it is time to head off for a local walk.

First colours walk

Choose to walk somewhere local where you will be able to look easily at plant growth. Set off with your camera (and notebook if you wish) and observe and photograph the colours you see. Pay attention to where exactly the colours are to be seen. Look at the ground around plants and trees, at branch tips, plant stems and anywhere you can see a hint of colour, growth or swelling. Are there any spring bulbs in flower yet? Are the tips of the trees or plants showing colour yet? What colours can you see? How would you describe them in words? I suddenly became aware while walking that red is the first really bold colour of spring in my locality. Is this observation true where you live? Or does some other colour catch your eye first, or more intensely?

Look, too, at how the colours are distributed: is there perhaps an even scatter of dots, or are there single bright flowers, bands of colour, groups of flowers, or clusters of green marks within still-dormant hedges and woods? Look for bands or areas of colour within the yellow-greens and browns of winter trees. As you walk during this period you will notice the colours becoming stronger over time, the dots getting bigger and the bands of coloured new growth extending. Willows, for example, often have a flush of orange at the ends of their branches creating a band of colour as if the branches have been dipped in paint. On other branches the new growth is a brilliant red. Note the intensity of the red colour and the sharp edge between the new red growth and the pale brown older wood in the photograph of a sycamore tree opposite.

Branches tipped with
red beside the
River Slea, Sleaford

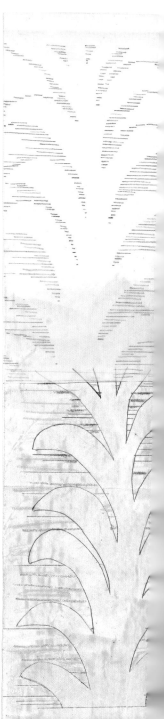

Left: *Pattern 255* Tree
of Life motif with
a template and stencil

Below: Various paperworks
based on *Pattern 255*

Exploring first colours

Once back home, begin by choosing one of the spring colours
you have observed during your walks, perhaps a yellow, orange
or red. Then choose a simple image of a growing plant from one
of your photos, or a book, or you could draw your own. Perhaps
one of your photographs could be printed out and a spring flower
or plant shape traced to provide you with a pattern to make a
template or stencil.

I developed my design from the abstracted plant pattern numbered
255 in the 18th-century Mary Ware notebook, now held at the
Bradford Textile Archive (see Chapter 5, pages 114–115). The sense
of movement provided by the curve of the stem fitted with the
sense of upward energy at this time of year. Pattern 255 probably
dates from the 1790s and is still appealing today.

Mark your image onto paper using your template or stencil. Then
fill in the space around the plant motif with vertical stitches or
vertical pencil/pen/crayon marks. The illustration will give you
some ideas. The marks can be angled or overlapped to give a
cross-hatched effect if you wish. Try using marks of the same
or varied lengths and thicknesses. Ensure that you fill the space
around the image, working to the edge of your fabric or paper.
Keep experimenting until you find a design you like.

MOTIFS FROM THE NATURAL WORLD

Makers of traditional British quilts and folk art used many motifs
derived from their surroundings and lives. Leaves, plants, spirals,
flowers, feathers, shells and many more motifs can be seen in quilts
held in museum and other collections. If this idea appeals to you,
look out for whole cloth quilts from the north of England and Wales.
The Quilters Guild development project documenting British quilts
during the 1990s led to the book *Quilt Treasures*. Now reissued, the
book contains a wealth of information including some useful pages
with examples of single motifs and use of patterns. Increasingly
textile collections are at least partly accessible online, offering
a wider variety of ideas to draw from. See Chapter 6 for some
starting points.

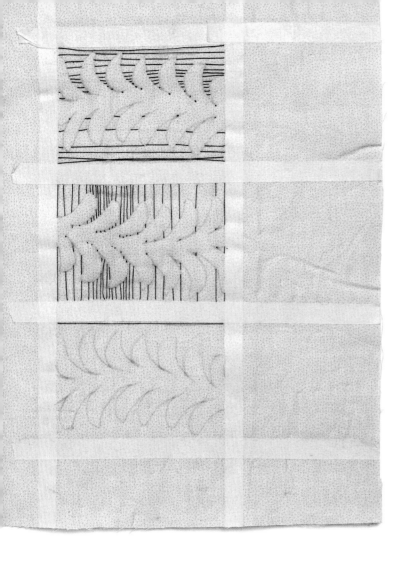

Exploring the first colour in hand stitch

Above left: Sample showing blue pen marking and three stages of stitching

Above right: *Pattern 255 repeated in long hand stitches*

Opposite: Sample using different thicknesses of thread

Mark your chosen design onto a top fabric using a suitable marker pen or pencil. Add a light wadding or fabric layer and a backing and begin to stitch using your paperwork to guide you.

Variation can also be introduced by using threads of various thicknesses. The sample, right, shows some variations using different red and white threads.

Going further: bands of colour

There is a very strong sense of upward and outward energy in the vibrant and vigorous new growth at this time of year. Some of this upward feeling and energy has been evoked for me by the use of vertical marks and stitches in the previous samples. I also wanted to explore how to express the energy of pushing outwards with bands of colour as seen in the image of willow heads on page 34. For this I turned to the idea of building up individual stitches pushing out from a central point in a banded radiating pattern.

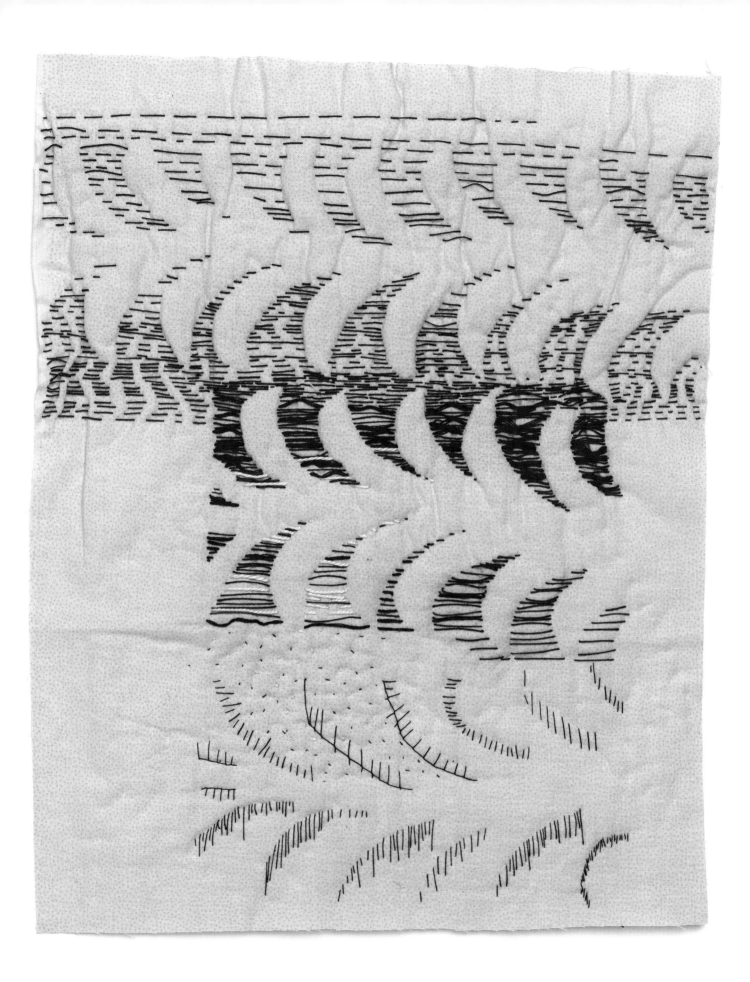

33 Spring

This approach works well with three layers of fabric, which will provide the necessary stability for the density of stitches. The diagrams show how the stitches can be built up steadily, always working from the centre outwards. Once the stitches in the base green colour were completed, further, coloured stitches were added to some of the radiating bands.

The completed stitched textile piece *Red is the First Colour of Spring*, shown on pages 36–37, blends several of the ideas in this section of the book.

Detail of willow heads
in spring

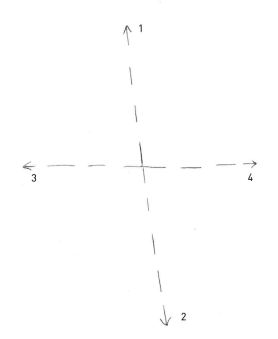

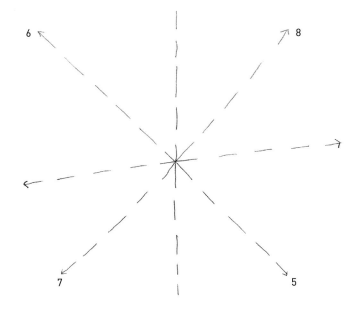

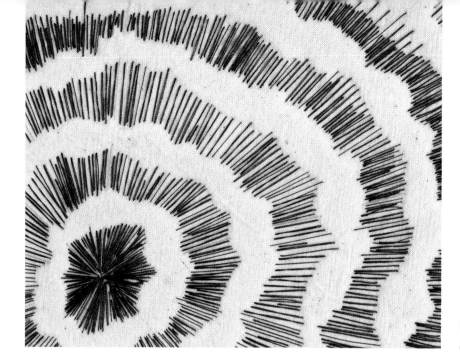

Detail of *Red is the First Colour of Spring*

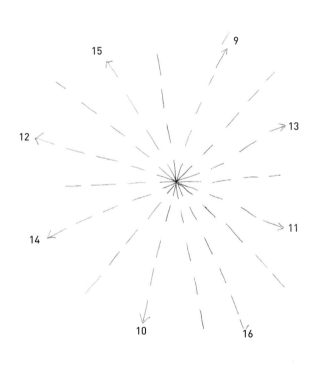

15

9

13

12

11

14

10

16

Above and left:
Diagrams for working radiant stitch

Left: Alternative stitch pattern

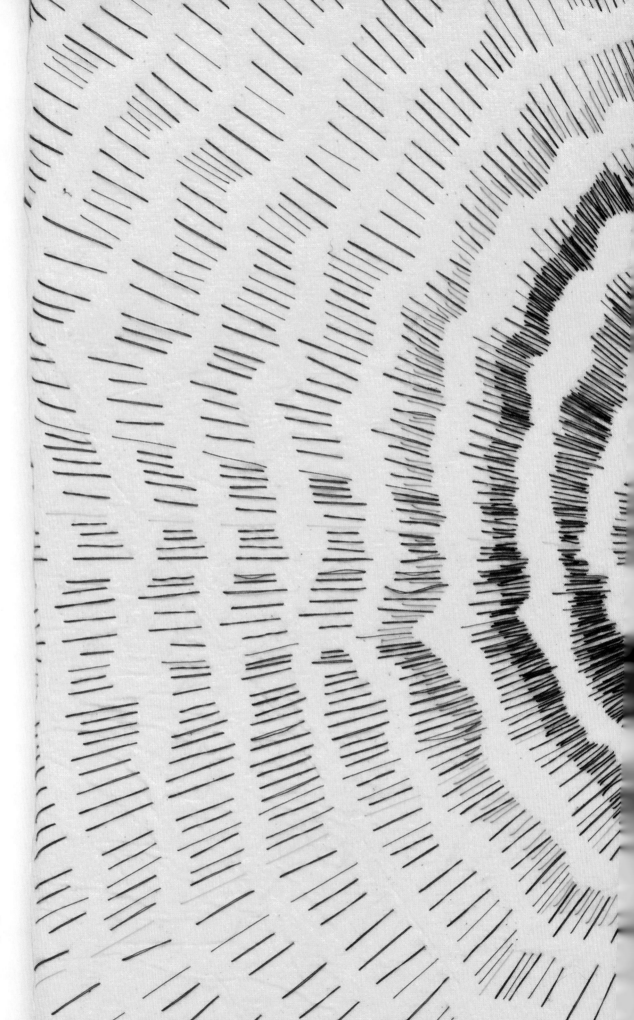

*Red is the First
Colour of Spring*

Equinox: light and dark

As the spring equinox draws closer, the balance between the hours of daylight and darkness continues to change, reaching an equal balance at the equinox itself. The increasing hours of daylight make it easier to spend more time outside walking, noticing and sketching. I am always relieved to be able to be outside more and often walk frequently at this time of year, impatient for more sunlight and pleased to reconnect with places a little further from home. The walk in this section focuses on observing light and dark.

Light and dark walk

Below left: Light and dark on a riverside, Derbyshire

Below right: Willow heads over the River Slea, Lincolnshire

Set off with your camera into your local park, woodland or fields to observe the different proportions of light and dark around you. This could be the balance of light and dark colours as seen in the leaves of a variegated plant for example, or the balance of a light sky with dark land, or pale water and dark rocks. Stand or sit and look for a while, observing your surroundings, including the light and the

passing weather. What attracts you? Wait for an opportunity or idea to form in your mind before you start to take any photographs. Consider the delicacy and softness of the new plant and tree growth, the warmth of sunlight on your body, new scents and the changing sounds as the world around you continues to reawaken.

Exploring light and dark marks

Gather together all the photos from your spring walks and look at what you have chosen to photograph. Does light or dark predominate? Are any types of mark recurrent? Are you attracted to the same type of mark over and over again, or are your photographs more varied than that? If so, how do they differ?

Try sketching your marks on paper to clarify your thinking, aiming to develop a mark that excites you. Once you have a stitched mark that excites you, choose a colour to work with. The next few paragraphs take you through an example of one of my ways of working from a photograph of marks to develop a finished stitched textile. The intention is that, having seen my approach, you can apply this to your own choice of mark.

Exploring light and dark in stitch

Worked example: five-point stitched mark

The photograph of willow heads from the previous section was still in my mind when I began this piece of textile. The way the individual stamens, with their light and dark parts, reach out into space from the centres offered inspiration for creating coloured marks by working stitches radiating out from a central point. I began by working directly in hand stitch on layered fabrics with a range of thread types in colours that I connect to spring. I wanted to find a simple mark that evoked vigorous outward growth. What evolved was a five-pointed mark blending the willow head example shown earlier with a simple plant seen growing on a spring walk. The samples that follow show how this simple mark was developed into a final wall-hung textile piece.

In the sample on page 41 the dark green 'arms' of the mark have been extended using thread in a second colour, namely orange. Notice what an impact this small addition of colour makes. The use of orange in this way links back to the earlier observation of seeing orange tips on willow trees and bands of colour at the very start of spring. This was my final test sample before using a long darner needle to hand stitch the two small round pieces shown on pages 42 and 43.

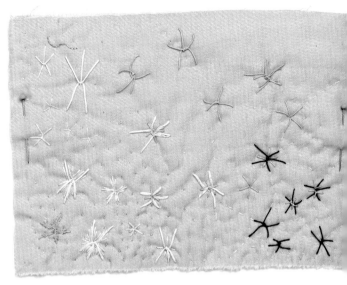
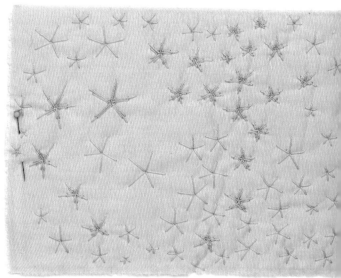

Sequence of samples showing the development of the five-point stitch mark

Equinox Light and Dark

In seeking to echo my observations of the balance of light and darkness at the equinox, my aim was to make a pair of related stitched images, not identical ones. I often plan my finished works in some detail, including marking out the designs. On this occasion spontaneity and trusting the process seemed a better fit for springtime energies. The two round pieces shown overleaf were stitched directly onto layers of fabric and stretched over frames once the stitching was completed.

I decided to make one piece using a light green cotton fabric stitched with dark green threads and the second piece using a dark green figured wool fabric with pale green thread. The top layer of fabric, a wadding and a base layer were lightly tacked together before I began stitching. I was aiming to reach a visual balance of background and repeated stitched marks that felt 'right' to me. The pair of works would be completed when they were 'ready'.

Exploring working directly into fabric

Stitching directly means not planning and marking where the stitches
will go before you start. Explore this by choosing a mark or marks to
experiment with, then gather some fabrics for a sample. Begin with a
light fabric and a selection of dark threads. Use three layers of material:
the pale top fabric, a background fabric and a wadding layer, and cut
each at least 30cm (12in) square. Working on this scale enables bolder
marks and stitching. Place your chosen three layers together, with the
wadding in the centre, ensuring that the edges are lined up, and then pin
or tack the layers to hold them together.

Green/orange
sample with the long
darner needle

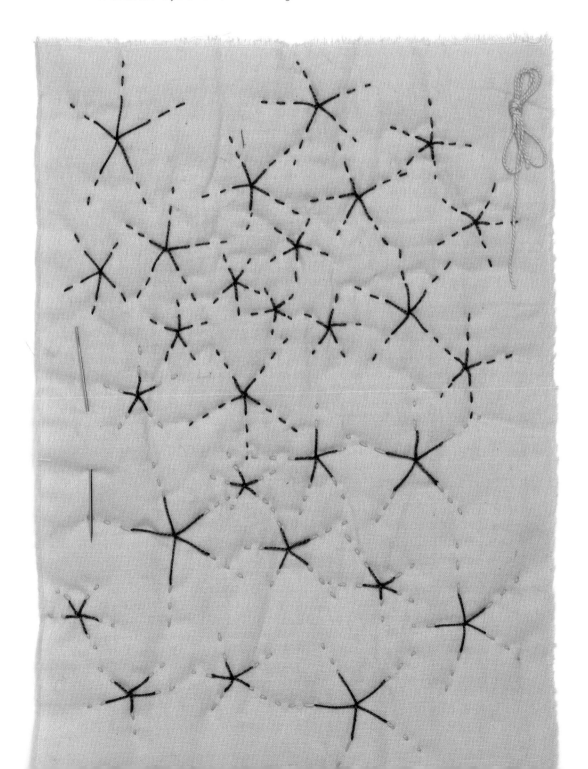

Equinox Light and Dark
round panels

Select a bold thread and a suitably sized needle for the thickness of the thread, and then start stitching in the centre of your sample. Experiment with how you could stitch your chosen mark and the spacing between the marks, and explore how a pattern could be developed. Pay attention to what you like and do not like. Stay with the ideas you like most and keep stitching. Working directly (without guide marks) onto the fabric will give a freer result than if the stitches are marked out first. You are aiming for around half the surface area to be stitched, leaving the remainder unstitched. Knowing when to stop stitching is important. If you are not sure if you have finished yet, stop and fold the raw edges under, then put the piece up on a wall. Walk past the piece from time to time and notice where any additional stitches might be needed to create a satisfying balance.

My final textile artwork here, *Spring/ Summer Yellow/Green Radiant*, blends and integrates several of the ideas I have shared so far in this chapter: radiating growth, pushing strongly outwards, subtle colour, slanting light and lines of germinating seeds. The development samples are shown on pages 104 and 105.

Below: Detail of *Spring/Summer Yellow/Green Radiant* wall-hung quilt

Right: *Spring/Summer Yellow/Green Radiant*

Expanding colour

This section looks at expanding colour during the transition from late spring into summer, the time around May Day. After the spring equinox, daylight becomes more and more dominant and the days brighten. The landscape changes a great deal during this time. The vegetation that has been growing apace continues to grow steadily, expanding and filling out local gardens, parks and the wider landscape.

The visual details and effects of expanding colour vary locally. Each plant will have a specific sequence of growth, opening, flowering and dying back. In England the bluebell is one of the most celebrated of spring flowers. A woodland plant, the bluebell grows and flowers before full leaf cover is established in the trees above. There are only a few weeks in which to visit these flowers as they pass through their various subtle and entrancing stages of growth, bloom and decay. Visually, bluebells can be a scatter or cluster of blue dots hovering among bright green leaves, seen through tree trunks or a broad glade of intense blue, depending on the setting. Often the landscape is transformed by this seasonal magic. Walking in the same woodland in the winter is often very dull by comparison. Consider what the significant flowers and plants are in your locality at this time of year.

The pieced quilt by Susan Denton illustrated overleaf is titled *Bluebells II, Full Bloom*. It is one of a sequence of quilts exploring the stages of growth and decay of bluebells in woodland. Beginning with *Bluebells I, Just Starting*, the sequence ends with *Bluebells III, Nearly Over*. The use of vertical strip piecing echoes the vertical tree trunks and the flashes of blue seen between them. The use of the same piecing technique to create a series of related quilts provides a framework, while the colours, layout and fabrics change for each quilt.

Observing expanding colour
The walk and explorations that follow are based on the idea of colour expanding across a plainer ground.

Bluebell

Expanding colour walk 1

Late spring is a good time look at the broad landscape and its colours. Field crops are often interestingly coloured at this time of year. In the UK crops, such as oilseed rape, become vivid expanses of intense colour, changing the wide views of the countryside for a few weeks with their field-sized patches of brilliance. The distinctive acid-yellow colour of oilseed fields becomes more dominant as the plant moves from bud into flower, and the blue-grey-green leaf and stem foliage is overshadowed by the developing flowers.

For this walk, if you can, go somewhere with fields of crops or pasture, open woodland or meadows. You could perhaps visit a fruit orchard, or walled garden, to spark some new ideas. These managed landscapes can be very beautiful with their blossoming fruit trees, orderly layouts of vegetable plants and scented herb gardens.

Above left: Horse chestnut branch coming into leaf, Porter Valley, Sheffield

Above and left: Bluebells in Ecclesall woods, Sheffield

Set off with your camera on a sunny day to observe and take photographs of massed plants in flower. Focus on the colours around you and where they occur. Look within the expanses of green for dots of a single colour or for bands and clusters of colours. Take lots of photographs, concentrating on the colours you see, how and where they occur.

Record your experiences and observations in photographs, with some notes and sketches if you wish. Sometimes a few quick words jotted down can most accurately evoke something you have seen or felt when you return to it later. Wherever you choose to go, find time to look out and across your surroundings, noting the ongoing changes as spring moves into summer.

Once back at home, look at your photographs and consider how well they capture your experience of seeing and being among the plants. My experience is that my photographs rarely properly capture the intensity of the experience of seeing the strong colour and massing of flowers. My eyes are so much more sensitive to what I am seeing than my camera is. With bluebells for example, there is often a horizontal blur of blue, visible at a distance, shimmering in the light, which cannot be easily captured in a photograph. These memorable effects can be very fleeting and elusive.

Expanding colour walk 2
After reviewing your photographs you may be inspired to go for another walk and take more photographs of the massed flowers to try and better reflect your own visual and sensory experience. Alternatively you may wish to experiment by choosing another flowering plant, or the same type of flowering plant observed and recorded in a different setting. Perhaps taking a sequence of photos of your chosen flowering plants at weekly intervals in your local park will work for you.

Exploring expanding colour

Back at home, edit your digital photographs to remove those that are less useful, then separate out some close-up views of groups of one type of flower. Look for the photographs that most closely reflect your experience. What aspects of the close-up photographs attract you: a colour, a repeated form, a line, a band, a shape? You may find it helpful to print out some of your digital photographs at a small size for ease of comparison and decision-making.

Bluebells II, Full Bloom,
Susan Denton

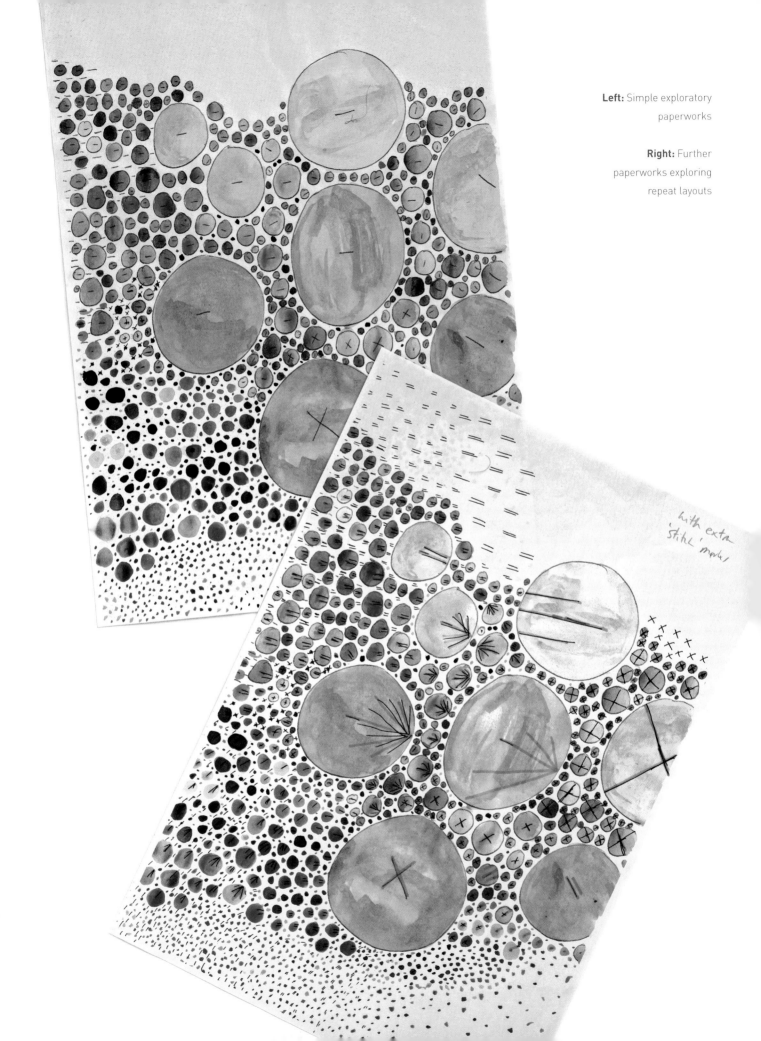

Left: Simple exploratory paperworks

Right: Further paperworks exploring repeat layouts

with extra 'stitch' marks

Worked example

I chose to explore the massed flowering bluebells I had glimpsed through the ancient tree trunks in Ecclesall woods. At the time I was also researching 18th-century textiles, including the use of sequins and spangles in luxury clothes. I began to consider the idea of adding a mass of bluebell-inspired sequins to a luxury fabric ground. In my choice of collage and appliqué for exploring this theme I sought to evoke the richness and intensity of my experience of walking through massed bluebells at this time of year.

I began to draw sequin-type shapes in curved bands across sheets of paper. Then I photocopied the sheets of marks and began to colour them in with blue watercolours. I drew extra marks to explore possible layouts for appliqué and stitching.

These initial paperworks were then colour photocopied and cut into rectangular and triangular sections, which I combined in different ways to explore creating a massed effect using repeat patterns as I sought to find a 'right' way forward for my idea.

Using the examples and working from your own photographs as inspiration, make simple drawings of marks expanding across sheets of paper. Your choice of mark could be a circle, as used here, or another small organic shape taken from your photographs. Perhaps you have a favourite shape you often use that could be explored further here.

Expanding colour: making sequins

Select a range of background fabrics, papers and thin plastics to cut into small shapes to make sequins. Explore using opaque and translucent plastics recycled from milk bottles and drinks bottles. Pieces of plastic can be cut out of the curved bottle shape and then hand-cut to make curved sequins. Some plastic bottles have seam lines and textured areas that can be interesting to include when cutting the sequin shapes.

Begin to arrange the sequins on fabric backgrounds in different ways, then stitch them down with straight stitches, varying the placing of the stitches as you explore what is possible when working with these materials and this technique.

Exploring further

Use permanent markers to colour or add marks to the recycled plastic before cutting out the sequin shapes. Try cutting a range of sequins in different shapes; petal and leaf shapes, oblongs

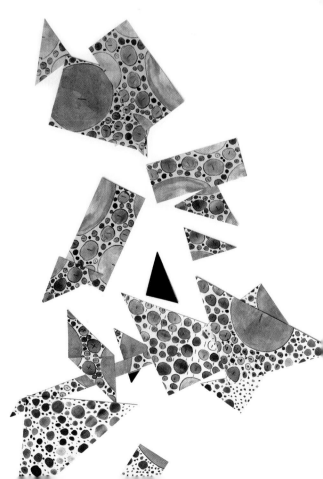

Examples of coloured and marked plastic pieces to make sequins

and ovals. Arrange the shapes and stitch them down in different patterns. Try different types and thicknesses of thread to attach the sequins to add further visual and textural variety.

This idea could be explored further in several ways, for example by making work that is specifically related to issues of environmental sustainability or work focused on the use of sequins in historic court dress and accessories.

Enjoy the Spring!

Spring is a wonderful season with so much visual excitement for an artist to work with. Walking in springtime can offer many fabulous and inspiring experiences. The themes and ideas I have shared here are only some of the myriad possibilities for making distinctive textile works inspired by spring.

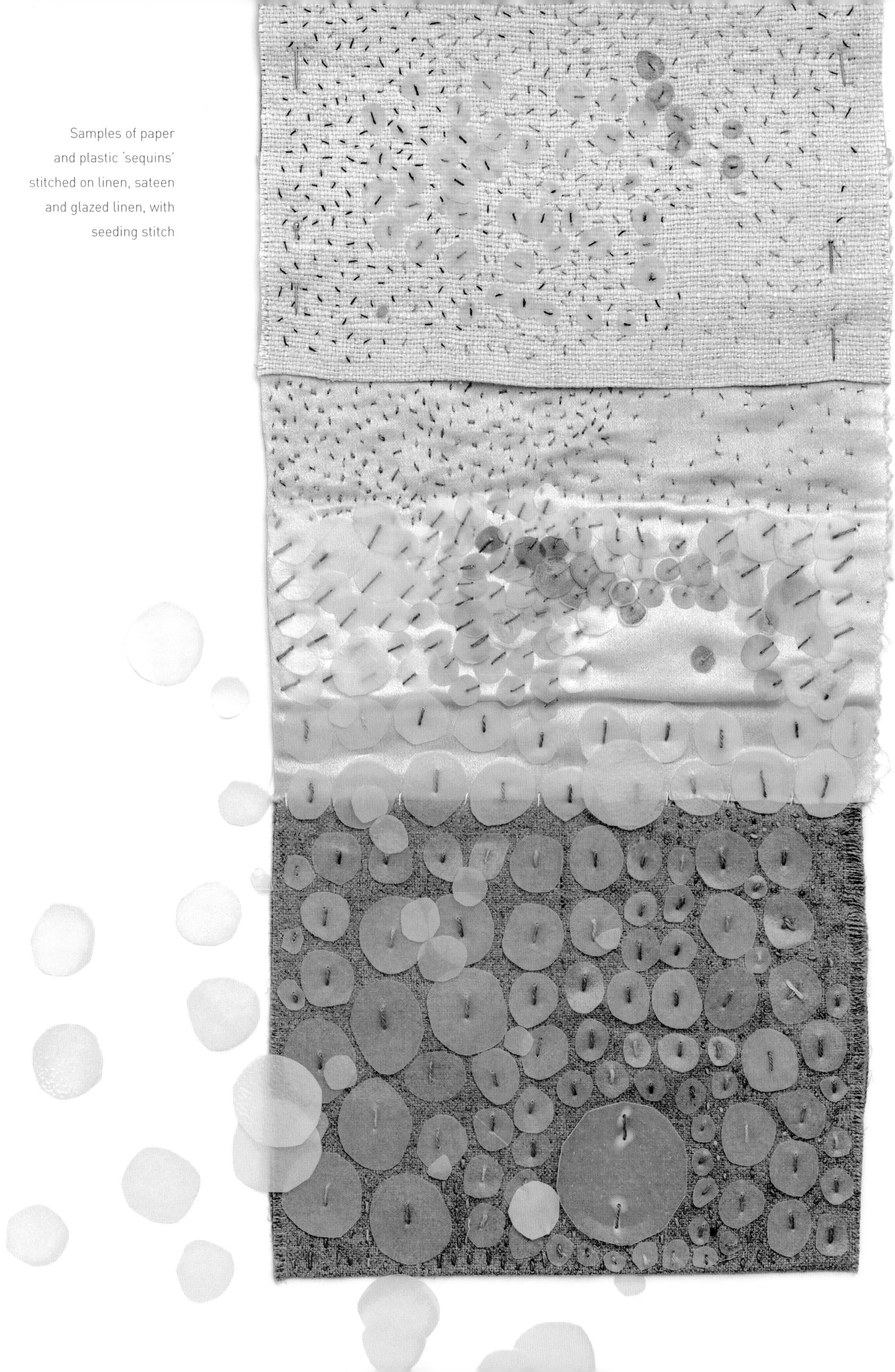

Samples of paper
and plastic 'sequins'
stitched on linen, sateen
and glazed linen, with
seeding stitch

CHAPTER 2

Summer

As spring moves into summer, the seasonal energy is stronger and steadier with a feeling of continuing expansion. The trees and plants fill out, meadows and gardens move into their full flowering. Altitude subtly influences these changes. The meadow photograph shown here was taken quite close to the date of the summer solstice (21 June), at a high and cool location where the plants flower later than near my home.

Summer meadow,
Castleton, Derbyshire

Summer is a favourite time of year for many people, offering many different potential sources of inspiration. The longer summer days also offer more opportunities for easier travel locally and further afield. Ideas for creative ways of working when away from home are included in Chapter 5 (see page 107).

I have chosen two of the many aspects of summer to provide a focus for walks and studio-based explorations, namely midsummer and harvest. The section on midsummer covers the time either side of the June solstice and the section on harvest covers the period after that until summer comes to a close. These two phases of summer can last over many weeks, sometimes overlapping with each other, sometimes fading gently from one to the other, always with subtle variations related to altitude.

Stellate Meadow work based on summer meadows, drawing on the development process for the five-pointed stitch mark

Midsummer

An English summer can be a very variable experience. One year there might be days and days of bright sunshine and blue skies, while in other years there may be much rain and many storms. All these variations offer creative potential. After all, it is much easier creatively to respond to what happens around you, than to decide that this is the year you will focus on the brilliant midsummer sunshine, only to experience above-average rainfall and flooding!

Whatever the summer weather, the colours of the landscape continue to change around me. The leaves of the trees grow and block daylight from reaching the woodland floor. All the trees and plants continue to develop, blooming, darkening and maturing. In my locality, this is the time of year when the wide range of shades of pale, vivid greens seen in the spring trees have mostly faded to a more uniform shade of mid to dark green, as seen in the photograph of a single sycamore tree in summer, opposite. From a distance much of the woodland looks a similar green, and walking in the woods is a cool and shady experience contrasting strongly with the daylight outside.

Midsummer trees walk

With the sharpness and brightness of the spring greens gone and the glorious colours of autumn yet to come, the shapes and textures of midsummer trees are the focus of this walk. As well as walking in the countryside, walking in city parks and suburban streets can be good for observing and photographing the shapes, textures and foliage of interesting looking trees and plants. With this in mind, consider taking a walk along tree-lined streets or in a botanical garden or arboretum.

As you walk, take lots of photographs, looking at single trees and their overall shapes. Notice whether the tree is 'open grown' (with an evenly filled out and symmetrical shape) or if its form has been distorted by closeness to other trees, traffic, buildings or by a strong prevailing wind. Trees and hedges on hilltops and near the coast often show this prevailing wind effect most clearly in their

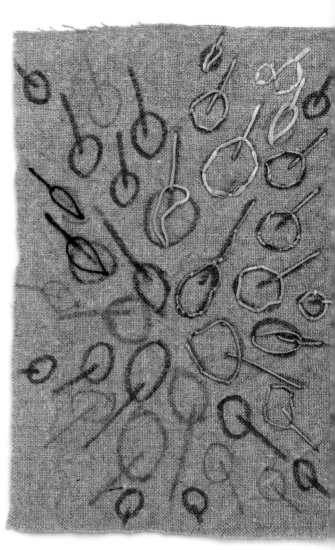

angled and asymmetrical forms. Also look at damaged trees and those felled by strong winds. Take time to look at the textures of the foliage of the trees. Are the leaves still thin and smooth to the touch, or are they more solid and heavily ribbed now? Are they blotched and textured in places, perhaps by insect activity? If you can find a convenient seat near a tree with interesting foliage, take the opportunity to sit down and look slowly and thoroughly at the leaves and their textures. Think about how the textures and shapes you see – photograph and touch could inspire your stitching.

Exploring midsummer trees through stitch

After a local walk one midsummer, including time spent observing the isolated sycamore tree shown above, I returned home with an idea. A sample of detached chain stitch previously made in response to a visit to Australia resonated with me and this idea. The leaf shape here related well to the tree idea.

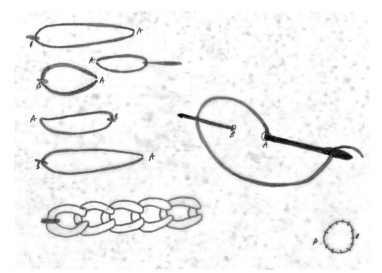

WORKING CHAIN STITCHES

- Bring the thread up at A where you want the base of the stitch to be. Hold the thread to the left with your left thumb while you insert the needle back into hole A, keeping a loop of thread on the surface.
- Bring the point of the needle up at B where you want the end of the loop to be. Gently pull the rest of the thread through, with the thread behind the needle.
- Adjust the size and shape of the loop to suit your idea.
- Make a straight stitch to secure the loop and pull the thread through to the back. If the loop is large, several straight stitches may be needed to hold the loop of thread in position.
- Secure the chain stitch on the reverse with a small back stitch and then bring the point of the needle up where the next detached chain stitch is to begin.
- Chains of stitches can be made by starting the next stitch within the loop of the previous stitch. Keep stitching until the chain is complete then secure it with a small stitch at the end.

My experience of the texture and shapes of summer trees came together in my mind with the earlier sample to offer a way forward. I worked directly in detached chain stitch onto fabrics layered with wadding to create the examples of tiny trees shown here. Beginning with the idea and stitch interlinked in this way is a different approach, without any development paperwork at this stage. I liked my initial results and began to explore the idea of detached chain stitch further.

Now do the same by developing a small introductory sample. Begin by choosing some natural-fibre threads and fabrics in unexpected and contrasting colours. Layer your choice of top and bottom fabric with a thin wadding, perhaps fleece or felt. Creating trees in this way is quite slow so I suggest beginning with a sample of around 20cm (8in) square.

Working with contrasting colours of fabric and thread will enable you to see the shape of the stitches better as you get to know what detached chain stitch looks like, how it can be built up and whether you enjoy stitching it or not. Once you have got to grips with making the stitch itself, try placing and massing the stitches to create flowers, patterns and trees as shown in the green strip sample overleaf.

When I felt familiar enough with making detached chain stitch to create trees, I decided to use the technique as part of a large-scale piece of textile work I was developing. It was only at this point that I needed to create paperworks to think through how I would place the stitch marks to express my idea. The paperworks and detail of the final work shown will give you some ideas for working in this way.

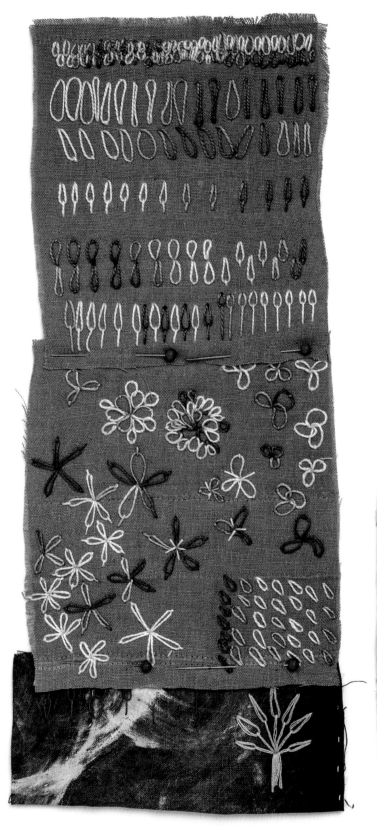

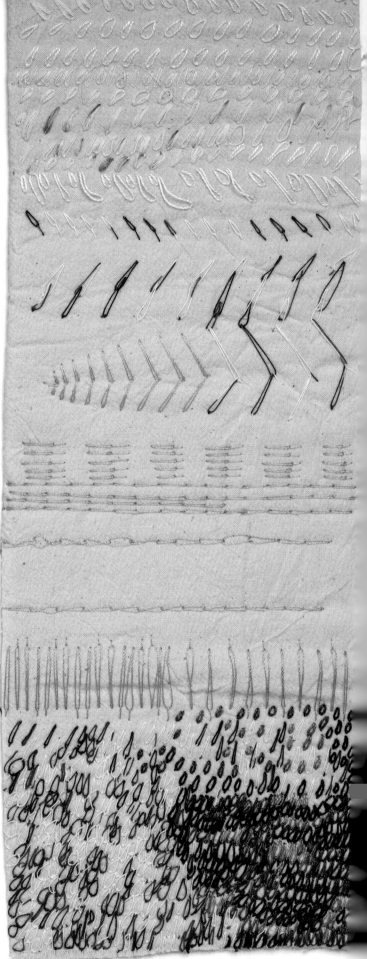

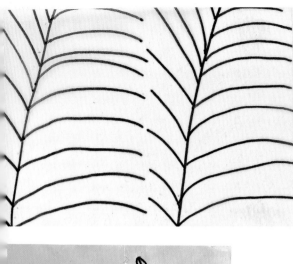

Above: Paperworks based on trees

Left: Samples of detached chain stitch

Right: Detail of tree from *Nine Yards or Thereabouts* quilt

Harvest

Late summer and harvest can be a time of abundance, ease and relaxation. This mood is reflected in the approach taken with the examples in this section. The landscape before and after the picking and harvesting of fruit, berries, vegetables and other crops looks and feels different again. Walking in your locality will enable you to connect to your local seasonal context, exploring what grows wild and is cultivated near you, how it is picked, harvested, collected and stored by people, birds and animals preparing for winter.

Harvest walk preparation

Inspired by this mood of ease, take the opportunity to prepare gently for this walk. Over a few days, mull over where you might want to go and walk. Where could you walk and see fruit, berries, vegetables and crops ready for harvest or already harvested?

In planning my own harvest walk I was looking for wide-open fields to match the mood of abundance and expansiveness that this time of year evokes for me. I was looking for cereal-crop stubble, tall, dried grasses, hay or straw bales of different shapes and sizes, traditional cereal stooks, haystacks and other classic signs of a grain harvest. There is also a strong connection to childhood memories of walking fields of hard stubble stalks. This walk meant a car journey to arable fields some distance away from my home.

Once you have decided where to go for your walk, prepare your materials before you leave home. Gather a selection of linen, cotton and other matt fabrics and threads in the colours you feel you might want to use. If possible, ensure you include some fabrics and threads with sheen. Perhaps if metallic golds or purples, for example, are not colours you usually use, you could experiment with them now. It is often easiest to take some risks such as exploring new colours, fabrics and threads when you are feeling relaxed and at ease. Times of ease and play are when creative outcomes can be open-ended. Playing and exploring in this way is a great opportunity to gently move your ideas and techniques on.

Above: Collection of visual materials on the theme of harvest

Above and right:
Collection of
photographs from
my harvest walk

I prepared for my walk by collecting together visual materials, objects
and images on the theme of harvest that I had already. My chosen
colours were bleached khaki greens, oranges, straws, creams, golds,
tans and grey. My experiment here was to use metallic gold thread.

Harvest walk

Once you have selected a suitable destination, collect your camera
and notebook and set off. Inhale, go gently and easily, savouring your
surroundings, noticing how the light falls, observing the changing
colours as the sun moves and where the shadows are. Observe and
record the harvest around you. Look at the different characteristics of
any rows or lines, their layout, how the lines might echo the shape of

the land. Observe the distant and detailed textures and patterns created by the processes of harvest in the landscape. Feel the textures beneath your feet, listen to the crunch and crackle of the dry stubble stalks as you walk across them. See and feel the differing sizes and strengths of the stalks and stems in different fields. Notice the crop debris left behind in the fields. The earth can be dry and hard, it may be cracked in places or puddled in others. Look at the construction of any bales of hay or straw: how are they made, how are they placed in the landscape?

Notice, too, the colours of the various crops and seek out the subtly varied shades of bleached yellows, browns, greys and golds. If you can, gather a range of stems and stalks to bring home with you. Look for the beginnings of any berries or leaves turning colour; hints of the autumn soon to come.

The photographs in this section are from my harvest walk, taken on a day when the sun was not shining. The grey skies offered a less conventional and more inspiring view of the classic subject of harvest.

Exploring harvest

When you return to the studio, look at your photographs and notes and pick one photograph to explore further. The first photograph that catches your eye is fine – don't over-think your choice. Cut some of your prepared fabrics to squares of around 20–30cm (8–12in), select a top fabric, wadding and backing fabric, or use three layers of the same fabric type. Select a needle and thread and start stitching in whatever way occurs to you. A photograph of rows might suit lines of running or back stitch. For example, interpreting the photograph of bales placed at regular intervals across the landscape may need a square or round stitch mark as well as lines of running stitch. Wild berries will need a more random approach.

Exploring harvest in spiral stitch

I chose to use a close-up photograph of a round bale. These bales are made by being rolled outwards from a central point. I had previously developed a textured and raised hand stitch I call spiral stitch. When stitched as a flat spiral this stitch echoed the construction of the round bales. See the diagram on page 68 for how to do this.

The sample shows spiral stitch worked by hand and using a sewing machine. I experimented with how I placed the stitches to create rays; four, five or more rays using single and double threads.

Above left: Diagram of flat spiral stitch

Above: Quick sketch, photograph and spiral stitch samples on space-dyed recycled cotton sheet

As I worked with this group of images my idea evolved, leading to stitching the whole surface with flat spiral stitch, as shown in the completed *Sun Wheel* panel, opposite.

Further development

Harvest inspiration can be further explored in many other ways. Some examples are:

- Developing stitched-paper collage of regularly spaced circles into a larger scale wall piece based on the precision of harvest processes such as the baling of hay or straw.
- Selecting other shapes and patterns as a base to develop ideas.
- Creating a series of subtly different wall pieces.
- Making a whole cloth bed quilt, hand or machine stitched across the entire surface, inspired by the lines of stems, stalks and bales seen in the landscape after crops have been harvested.

Right: *Sun Wheel* panel

69 Summer

Above: Collages based
on the pattern of straw
bales in the fields

Right: *Sun Wheel* collage

CHAPTER 3

Autumn

The first signs of autumn often occur in my locality in late August. In the garden early one morning I notice a new sound, I pause and realize it is the rustling of leaves as their edges begin to dry and crinkle. The purple moorland heather is still in bloom and people are still away on holiday. Yet summer is turning to autumn. The brilliant flowers that drew my eye earlier in the year are mostly gone now and the abundance and fullness of summer is coming to an end. It is time to let go of the joys of summer and return home.

Red cotoneaster leaves

With my awareness raised, I watch for more signs of autumn coming. The leaves begin to change in colour, becoming a fascinating range of reds, pinks, ochres, dark greens, khakis and browns in endlessly varying and sometimes bizarre combinations. Along the hedgerows and sides of walls the mass of vegetation that has grown over recent months begins to die back, drying, curling and fading to many shades of brown and yellow. Some individual leaves and petals develop interesting blotched patterns in surprising colour combinations, as shown in the photograph on page 72. Leaf stalks, sometimes still vibrantly coloured, soften and droop downwards. The more durable structures of the plants and trees, such as their seed cases, become more visible as the weeks pass. Out in the hills, the landscape darkens, taking on a bronze cast, changing first in the driest, highest and most exposed places.

Autumn can be a long season with the equinox occurring early in the season. For some, the fading away of the year is a sad time, somewhat echoed by the falling leaves. For others, there are the joys of seeing the brilliant autumn colours and the opportunity to observe and record the processes of decay and renewal proceeding and changing from year to year. One year the drying process is drawn out and subtle, while another year autumn comes early with heavy crops of berries and rapid changes in the colours of the vegetation in August.

Autumn is a good time of year to think about the structures and patterns around us on all levels. I still find this a time of important new beginnings in my life and creativity. Perhaps it is all those years when September marked the beginning of the new school year that still echo for me. For some individuals, this particular season often marks a significant life change; attending a new school or college, enrolling for a creative course, or moving away from home. For others, the change of season and the pattern of life is less outwardly obvious, but potentially no less profound.

As you make journeys on foot, by bus or train, or as a car passenger, observe your landscape as it colours and changes around you, and notice the way that the underlying structures are revealed as the vegetation falls away. There is much to see during autumn and it is a good time to revisit familiar and favourite places close to your home. When you can, collect small autumnal items that attract you for their colours or structures: leaves, seed cases, stems, nuts, seeds and so on. These seasonal items are good to have around you as inspiration, especially when it is too wet or cold to go outside later in the year.

This chapter covers autumn as two separate themes: first colour; then structures and processes. In reality, of course, colour, structures and processes are inextricably linked as seen in the photograph of cotoneaster on page 72.

Autumn colour

Autumn colour walk

This time, set off to walk, with your camera (and notebook if you wish), somewhere where the details of trees and plants will be easily visible and accessible to you. Perhaps a look around your garden or that of a friend, or a visit to the local park, hedgerow, woodland or an allotment will offer a rich source of ideas. Taking detailed photographs is much easier and safer when you can get near enough to your subject to observe it well and frame your photograph as you wish.

As you walk through your surroundings, look for the ongoing changes of autumn colours, their combinations and the patterns and textures created. Think about patches or splodges of colour, blotches and mottling, the colours of berries, seeds, bark and stalks. Take lots of photos, looking for the bold and occasionally bizarre colour combinations to be found now, as seen in the leaves on a cherry tree on a suburban road on page 13, or the hydrangeas below.

While you are out, collect a few attractively shaped leaves to press when you get home. The unique irregularities in the shapes of real leaves help to create interesting templates and stencils. Place your chosen leaves between two tissues in a flower press or between the pages of a heavy book until dried out.

Hydrangea sepals

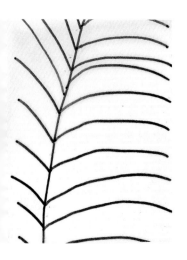

If you have time to take further walks during the weeks of autumn, take the opportunity to concentrate on just one aspect of colour. For example, you could look at variations on a single colour such as yellow or magenta, or you could choose to focus on observing and photographing particularly clashing, bold or unusual colour combinations. The photographs shown were taken very close to my home.

Exploring colours and leaf shapes

Back at home, assemble some coloured papers suitable for collage such as tissue and cartridge papers and some felt pens. Then begin to experiment with drawing repeat patterns based on leaf colours and shapes. Cut out the leaf shapes and place them in different layouts, gluing down any arrangements that you like. Try out some bizarre colour combinations, especially those beyond your usual colour choices. The examples shown will provide some starting points.

Once your pressed leaves are dry enough, draw round one of them on some thin card to make a template. Use the template to draw some leaf shapes on paper to cut out and experiment with.

Above: Initial
paperworks based on
simple leaf shapes

Left: Template drawn
from a pressed oak leaf
with paper cutouts

Far left: Horse chestnut
leaves with dried edges

Below left: Paperwork
based on leaf veins

The examples show paper collages with lines added to explore where stitching might be placed. Other ideas shown include quilting lines based on simple leaf shapes, a design for stitch based on the veins in the pressed oak leaf and cutouts made on a strip of folded paper.

Above: Paperworks
based on repeated
simple leaf shapes

Exploring appliqué

Gather your three layers of fabric, preferably lightweight cottons, to work on. The top layer should be a coloured and patterned fabric suited to the theme, while the middle layer of fabric works best as a contrast colour because it will show through the shapes cut out of the top layer. The backing can be a plain cotton fabric. An additional layer of wadding can be included if you wish. A square of around 30cm (12in) in each fabric or wadding is a good size for this sample.

Decide which of your designs you want to use, choosing the paperwork with the shapes that will make the most interesting cutouts. Trace or

Above: Detail of positive appliqué from *Nine Yards or Thereabouts*

Right: Reverse appliqué and echo quilting sample

mark your design on the top fabric and cut the shapes out carefully. Then place the cut-out fabric layer on top of the other fabric layers. Check you like the effect this creates with the contrast fabric you have chosen for the middle layer. Change the middle fabric if you wish. Pin and tack the layers together.

Starting in the centre, hand (or machine) stitch around the shapes through all the layers to hold them together. Make sure there are enough stitches to secure the cut edges of the leaf shapes and keep the sample flat. Once all the raw edges are stitched down, think about adding some quilting lines. The sample opposite shows lines of hand stitch placed at an increasing distance from each other. This is called echo quilting and it is inspired by the way that ripples spread out from a stone dropped into water.

Appliqué shapes can be considered positive or negative. The sample above is an example of a positive appliqué taken from the final textile work. The sample shown opposite uses the negative image from the same cut-out tree. The use of positive and negative images in this way also echoes the equal balance of hours of daylight and darkness at the autumn equinox.

Structures and processes

Autumn is a time for observing and reflecting on local views, structures and processes in the wider landscape. After time away during the summer, it is good to reconnect to my locality, seeing again the 'bones' of my local landscapes. The permanent buildings, hedges and walls, which were all hidden by the luxuriant foliage of spring and summer and thus unseen for months, now become visible again.

Think about the work of people in creating and maintaining the wider landscape and its structures over the centuries. If you are intrigued by what you see around you, you could take this interest further at your local library, museum or on the internet. Knowing more about what you are looking at, and the processes that created it, can be very satisfying and can deepen your connection to your locality. Specific buildings, street and field names can be a good place to start as they may record an earlier industrial process or aspect of life such as faith and education, or they may be named after a significant local person.

Much of my immediate locality has been influenced by small-scale industries and their processes, traces of which are still visible in some places. Examples include an unusually configured local building originally built as a brush factory, a nearby road called Button Hill named after the buttons that were made there in the 18th century and a farm up the hill called Smelting Farm, reflecting the earlier lead-processing industry.

Structures and processes walk 1

For this walk, plan to go somewhere where a wider view of your local area is possible. Look for broad views from the top of a slope, tall building or other high viewpoint that you can reach easily. If you can, take this exploratory walk on a bright and clear day so you can see for much greater distances.

Collecting your camera and wearing the right level of clothing for the altitude, set off for a walk. As you walk through your surroundings, look at the structures you can see now: walls, buildings, paths and other structures created by people. Think about any gates and fences you see and how they indicate the presence and absence of people and the processes of land ownership that created them. Take photographs of

Drying seed head

what interests you in this landscape of structures. You are aiming for a photograph that will remind you of what you saw at that moment. The actual quality of the photograph may not be great in terms of composition or focus. You may not be able to climb that tree or scale that wall for a really close look. These are photographs taken to prompt your memories, for your inspiration and use, not for sharing or for exhibition.

Make additional notes and sketches, while you are out or when you get home, to support your photographs if you find this approach useful. At this time of year the light may be poor, so my photographs and observations often benefit from a few notes of what inspired me, either at the time or when I get home. What matters here is to find a way of capturing what you see that suits you and will evoke what you have seen and felt whenever you wish to return to it.

Structures and processes walk 2

If you have the opportunity to go for a second walk, observe and photograph the detail of the autumnal processes of dying back and decay. Look at what is changing in both trees and plants, and where. Observe the first leaves to dry out and change colour. The changing leaves may be on one of the outermost branches of a tree, close to the trunk or at the very top. The pattern of change varies with the type of tree.

Sometimes the process of drying progresses in clearly visible stages, as seen on the seed head of this garden plant. The drier, open and browned seed cases are to the left, with the pale green full and rounded seed cases visible on the right. Here, drying has progressed from closest to the stem on the left outwards away from the plant. With other plants drying occurs first in the places most distant from the stem.

Exploring structures and processes

As a starting point, choose one of the photographs from your walks, which shows clear structures. With a pen, doodle some simple designs based on those structures on paper. This photograph of seed heads prompted me to doodle circular shapes as if seen from above.

Make a very direct copy of your doodles using fabric and thread in colours suited to the season. Make your hand or machine stitches freely as if you were drawing with a pen. Don't try to make a specific type of named stitch; instead, let the source photograph provide a guide for where to stitch. With practice this 'stitching as drawing' process gets easier and becomes more spontaneous. Here, I chose a bronzed green cotton and thin sewing threads to echo the colours of the season and the fragility of the seed head.

Developing this circular motif inspired me to try hand stitching circular and radiating motifs onto a commercially printed fabric. These experiments added richness and texture to the fabric, but the overall effect is more evocative of fireworks than of seed heads. This is a good sample to keep for reference for any future project inspired by fireworks.

The doodled seed-head idea could be developed as an embroidery or quilting motif, singly or repeated, on a small and delicate scale, or in a bigger and bolder way.

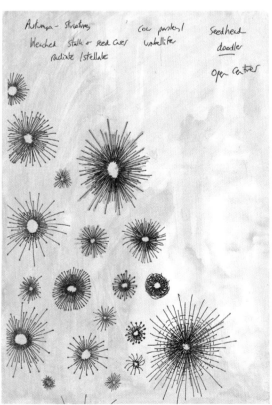

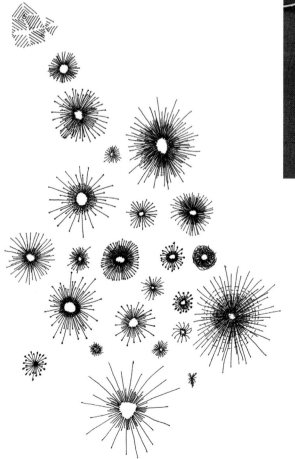

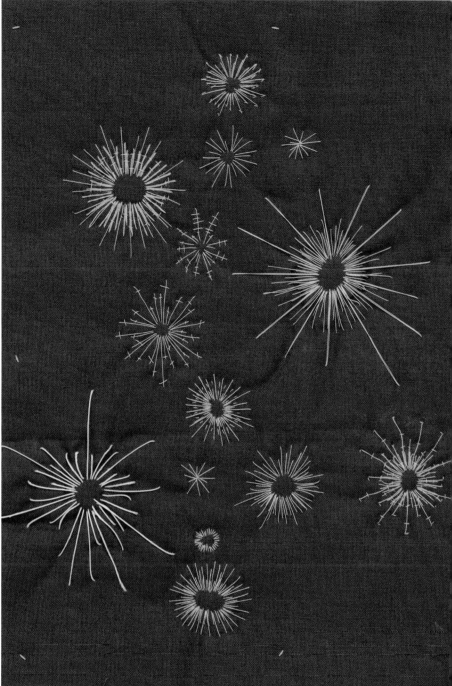

Top left: Pale bleached seed heads
of cow parsley

Above: Stitch sample based on doodles

Left: Two doodles based on skeletal seed heads

Far left: Hand stitch 'fireworks' motif variations
worked on commercially printed fabric

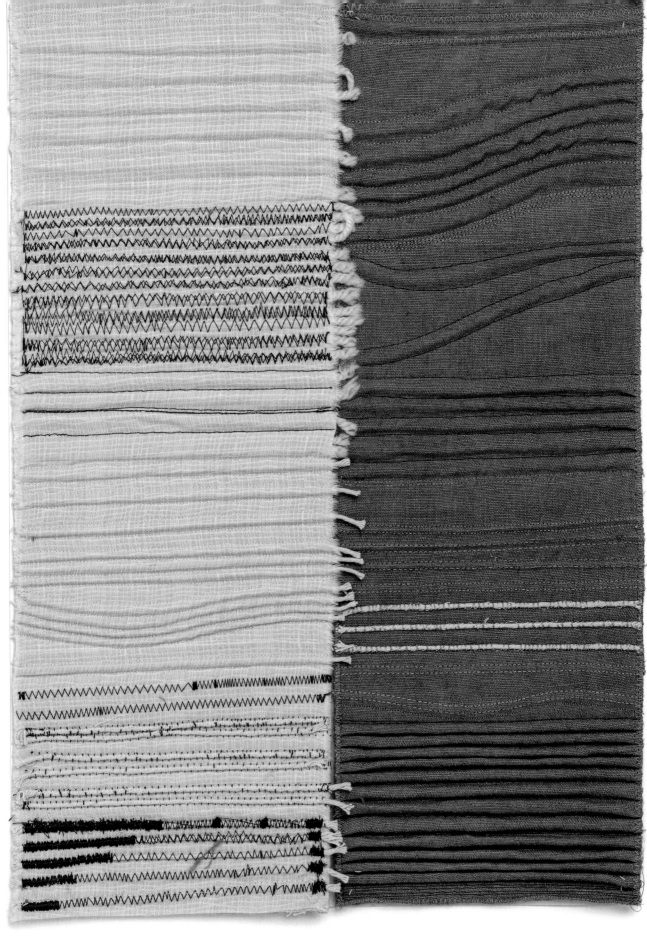

Above: Machine-stitched cording

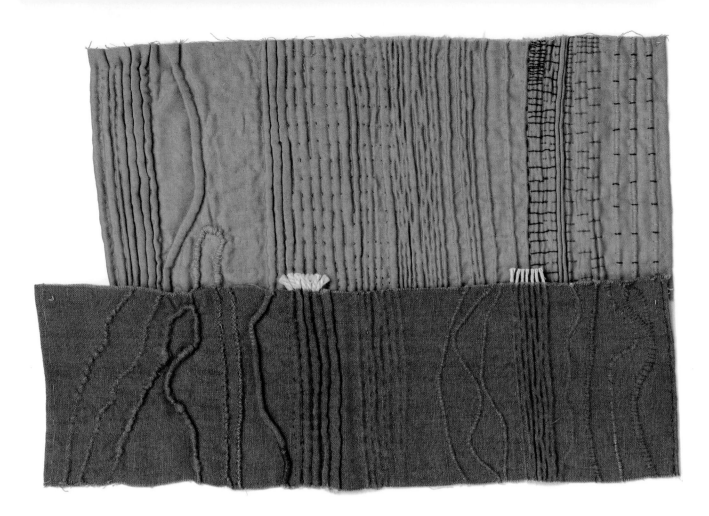

PLANNING A STRUCTURED SAMPLE PROCESS FOR CORDED QUILTING

Method: make four strip samples using different combinations of fabric, cord and stitch.

Hand stitched (above):

Strip sample hand stitched on gold curtain lining, left to right:

- Self-colour stitch corded with wool
- Coloured stitch corded with wool
- Self-colour stitch corded with cotton string
- Coloured couching stitches corded with cotton string

Strip sample hand stitched on grey-green linen, left to right (above):

- Self-colour stitch corded with wool
- Coloured and couching stitches, corded with wool.
- Self-colour stitch corded with cotton string
- Colour and couching stitches corded with cotton string

Machine stitched (left):

Strip sample machine stitched on grey-green linen (left), top to bottom:

- Self-colour stitch corded with wool
- Orange straight stitches corded with wool
- Self-colour stitch corded with cotton string, some string couched to top surface
- Orange straight stitches corded with cotton string

Strip sample machine stitched on a stiff yellow/white printed cotton (far left), top to bottom:

- Self-colour stitch corded with wool
- Coloured straight and zigzag stitch corded with wool
- Self-colour stitch corded with cotton string
- Coloured zigzag stitching and couching, corded with cotton string

A planned exploration of cording

One plant can inspire several different creative outcomes. The photographs here and on page 82 show stiff, vertically ridged stems against a stone wall. The hard-ridged stems inspired me to explore the new technique of cording. I had no earlier samples to draw on so I planned a set of four exploratory samples shown on the previous pages. The four samples used synthetic and natural fibre fabrics and different cording materials, stitched by hand and machine in a structured way.

These stems could inspire a wall-hung textile piece, perhaps in a thin vertical format. Alternatively, the stems could inspire a quilt made in bleached cotton fabrics with machine-stitched lines of varying widths, softly corded with wool in parts to raise some lines. Using machine stitching in this way could reflect the toughness of the stems as well as being a suitable method for making a functional item such as a bed quilt.

Parts of the cording samples could also be described as couching, because the securing stitches are visible on the top surface, rather than being hidden on the reverse. These stitches add further visual interest to the corded surface. The further sample of couching/cording (opposite) shows loose 'cords' of hand-spun and hand-dyed fleece hand couched to the background fabric, giving a very different result that could be further developed using more varied colours.

Above: Ridged stems of cow parsley

Making a planned sample

Planning and making a sample such as this is a useful approach when you are new to a technique. For this exploration, select a technique or stitch you are unfamiliar with and have thought you would like to try out. Alternatively, look at an encyclopedia of stitches or textile techniques for some new ideas. Work out your options on paper first, using my diagram as a guide, then set up your samples using layered fabrics and stitch away. If the technique or stitch you have chosen is a large one, make your samples larger than for a technique or stitch that gives a smaller result.

Exploring further
You could decide to explore new techniques, perhaps one each month during the coming winter, to broaden your textile vocabulary of fabrics, techniques, stitches and marks.

Right: Hand-spun and dyed wools couched with hand stitches. Wool dyed and spun by Karen Barrass

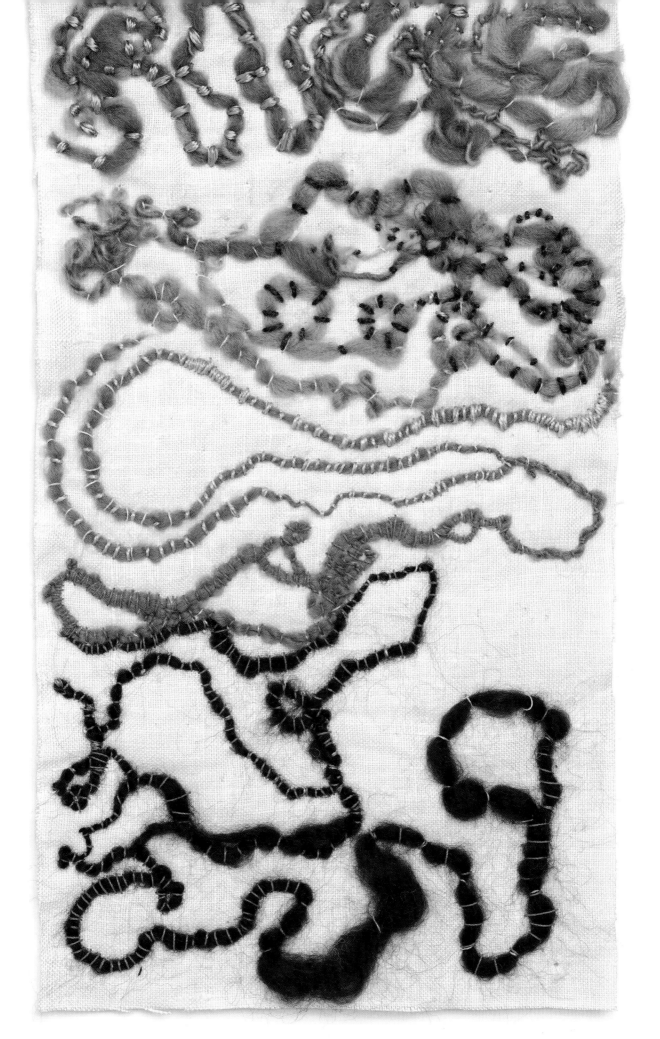

CHAPTER 4

Winter

- -

As autumn passes into winter and the midwinter solstice draws nearer, the hours of precious daylight decrease steadily. On some days it feels as if it never quite gets properly light at all. I change my routines to make the most of the limited light, often walking and taking studio time in the middle part of the day. I enjoy the vibrant late dawns and early sunsets. Often the smudgy line of the horizon at sunrise, like a stick of red or apricot pastel drawn horizontally across a textured handmade paper shaded with greys, inspires me for the day ahead. The sunsets can be spectacular too, as the deep red ball of the setting sun slips behind the horizon amid the dark silhouettes of trees and buildings in the fading grey light. Winter is a time of variability, often fast changing and surprisingly exciting.

Winter trees in the
Limb Valley, Sheffield

Above left: Rosehips in a storm
Above right: Ice at the edge of a moorland pond, Burbage Rocks

Some people have a real passion for winter: often it is the icy cold aspects that excite them, maybe the brilliance of the snow and ice, or the magical effects of hoar frost. What do you feel about winter? What colours do you see when you look carefully? How would you describe the quality of the light at the different times of a winter day? Is it hard and cold as in the image on page 88?

The walks in this chapter cover winter wet and winter cold. This split helps you focus your observations. Winter wet and winter cold may occur as two distinct and consecutive periods of times, but more usually they are interleaved. Rain, ice, frost, hoar frost, storms and snow may last over a period of hours or days, and sometimes several types of weather occur on the same day.

The wetness of winter intensifies and enriches the colours and details around me. Cold weather phenomena also bring fresh visual inspiration, offering potential for new insights and photographs of the local and familiar. It is worth going out to explore on some of these wet and cold days, camera in hand. Sometimes the weather conditions mean a short stroll round the garden or a local park is the most suitable option. The shapes of the larger, more architectural plants in gardens and parks can provide brilliant inspiration when glossy with rain, heavily rimed with frost or laden with snow.

Taking photos as a way of recording your observations is an activity well suited to this time of year as the rain, cold or wind conditions may not encourage much lingering.

Sound and light

This book is primarily about the visual world, but paying attention to all our senses while out walking, whether in an urban or a rural setting, can be very worthwhile. The mood and energy of a season is also created by the sounds around us. In winter, a walk undertaken when untouched snow is blanketing all around will be a very different experience to one undertaken when the sun is shining, temperatures are rising and ice and snow are thawing fast and noisily. Really long-lasting snowfalls can bring a special kind of silence and stillness.

Consider, too, the quality of the air and the light when you go for a walk. Is the air moving gently? Is it blustery or still? Is the day crisply sunny with a brilliant blue sky and a blueish light on the snow? Is the winter light dull, grey, heavy, misty, hazy? Is the light stable or is it changing from minute to minute? What effect is the time of day having on the light? Can you walk in the moonlight? What can you discern about tomorrow's weather conditions from today's walk? If you need some help to find the exact word to describe what you have seen and experienced try using a thesaurus to help you.

Solstice, around 21 December, is the time of maximum darkness and least daylight. Moonlight is more easily seen during these weeks, given the long nights, and it can be a very beautiful and subtle light to see the world by.

The settling in of winter encourages me to stay at home more. I begin to reflect on the year that has passed, the artworks made, teaching and experiences shared, the coming festive season and the importance of celebrating light to people in many cultures at this time of year. Time spent at home reflecting, mulling and thinking enables new connections and synergies to be made. This feeling of connection and synergy is reflected in a slightly different structure for this chapter. As before, there is a suggested walk for each of the chapter themes. Then there are two studio-based exercises in paper and stitch, which blend inspiration from both winter wet and winter cold.

Winter wet and cold

Frequent rain brings a sodden and heavy feel to the landscape. When the sun does shine, the few remaining coloured berries sparkle through the raindrops gathered on them. Deep, strong colours are to be found in the glossy wetness of the decaying autumn leaves and stems, the stones of the walls and in the still-growing green mosses, plants, lichens and algae.

Winter wet walk

After dressing appropriately for the wet weather, set off with your camera for a local walk. Look at the shapes of the trees: if you look closely maybe you will see that they are dotted with birds gathering to roost or resting in groups during migration. Notice, too, the intensification of colour that wetness brings. Details of the world are enhanced: tree trunks look glossy in parts, their colours deepened and enriched; walls can appear richly coloured and highly textured with mosses.

As you look out and across your surroundings, notice the ongoing changes of winter, especially the variety of colours and textures. Observe and record the colours and patterns you can see by taking photographs and making notes. If winter is not your preferred time of year, you may also notice and take heart from the first hints of spring in the buds and catkins sometimes visible.

Winter cold walk

Once you are dressed warmly for the weather conditions, set off with your camera for a local walk. Observe the light: is it pale, hazy or brilliant sunshine with blue skies? Pay attention to the unique, often fleeting effects of frost, snow and ice. Consider, too, the quality of the sound or stillness around you.

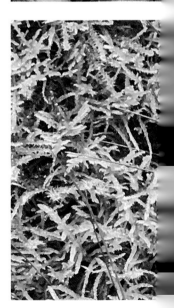

Here are some starting points for your observations:

Frost
Observe the way that frost makes shapes more visible, noticing its extent and range. Does frost occur only in some sheltered places or across the whole landscape? How thick is it and what type of frost is it? What happens as it melts?

Snow
A light covering of snow can illuminate tiny, rarely seen details, offering a new view of the familiar, perhaps revealing traces of previous human activity in the landscape such as settlements, mine workings or other archaeology.

The direction of the snow-bearing wind can sometimes be seen in a thin raised line of snow down one side of tree trunks and walls. Heavier snowfalls cover and smooth the familiar shapes of trees and buildings. If the snowfall continues for long enough it can obscure the shapes and muffle sounds. Look, too, for the tracks of animals and birds over fresh snow, revealing movements that are usually invisible and showing that our gardens and parks are shared with many others.

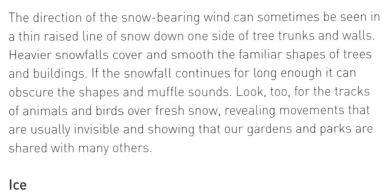

Ice
Where ice has been broken and refrozen on ponds over successive days and nights the angular and broken patterns can become increasingly complex. Notice, too, the gleam of ice lit by a low sun, especially if the ice has refrozen after snow melt across a wide area. As snow and ice melt and drip they may refreeze during the night, making icicles in beautiful and unusual shapes.

The white-on-white of snow and ice always remind me of the subtle white-on-white stitching of traditional English North Country quilts. Such quilts were often worked on a sateen fabric so the slight sheen of the fabric set the stitching off, as sunlight can illuminate an expanse of snow or ice.

Thaw
Observe the effects of melting ice; water making drip marks on dry surfaces, creating patterns as temporary streams speed down slopes and valleys, flattening vegetation and leaving debris caught in fences or against bridges. As snow and ice thaw, the landscape becomes coloured once more and there is often a bright white line of snow left on the shaded side of walls and buildings.

Top: Rain-soaked beech leaves

Centre: Herb robert and ivy growing by a wall near Abney, Derbyshire

Bottom: Bright green moss soaked by melting snow

Exploring winter wet and cold

Back in the warmth of your studio it is time to explore how the winter season inspires you.

Exploring broken ice

Find a few A4/A3 sheets of a type of paper that reminds you of snow or ice. Thin white office paper, tracing paper, watercolour paper or some reusable white plastic-coated packaging papers are all good to use here. Take one piece of your chosen paper and cut it into angular pieces inspired by photographs of patterns in broken ice. This is easily done with scissors, but if you prefer straighter and sharper lines, use a craft knife and a ruler instead.

Arrange and rearrange the paper shapes on a backing paper with gaps and overlaps. Once you have a layout you like, glue the paper pieces down. Allow the collage to dry, preferably under a weight or cutting mat to ensure it dries flat. Once the first collage is fully dry, cut it into angular shapes, then arrange these cut-paper shapes on another sheet of paper until you have a design you like and glue them down. Allow to this collage to dry, preferably under a weight or cutting mat. See the images opposite for some ideas.

Once it is dry, look at your collage and decide if you like as it as a whole. Or use two L-shaped pieces of paper to make a 'window' to separate off areas of the collage that you like and that offer potential to be developed further. Alternatively, repeat the cutting, arranging and glueing of the paper shapes a couple more times to reach a pleasing outcome, or begin a new collage.

This exercise can be repeated many times, giving increasingly complex results. Further variation can be introduced by the use of a strongly coloured backing paper. I combined this 'broken-ice' inspired collage method with my observations of patches of brilliant colour appearing on the ground beneath melting ice to develop the samples illustrated overleaf. These samples led to a pair of hand-quilted, wall-hung works: *Vice Versa 1* and *Vice Versa 2*, shown overleaf.

These two quilts, one with positive and one with negative patterns, are made of painted, cut out and collaged thermal-coated fabric (non-fraying), laid on white polyester wadding, scattered with tiny pieces of vivid-coloured threads, then trapped by a top layer of net and hand quilting.

Collage sequence inspired by refrozen ice

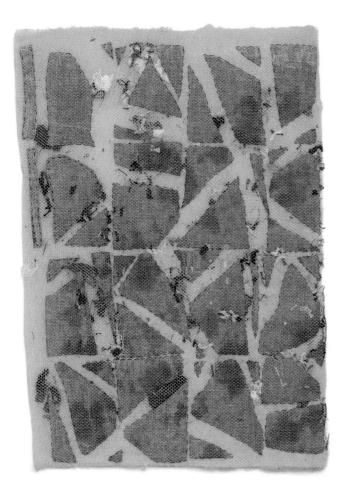

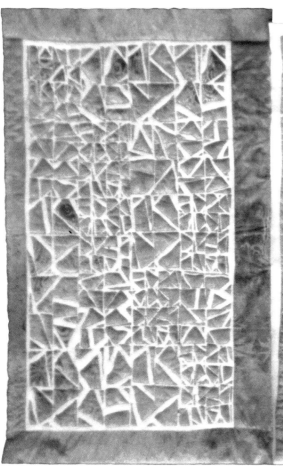

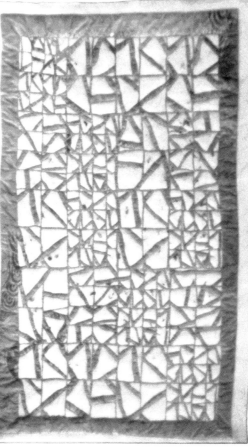

Above left: *Vice Versa 1* sample

Above right: *Vice Versa 2* sample

Left: *Vice Versa 1* and *Vice Versa 2* quilts

Right: Paperwork design development for *Comfort Blanket*

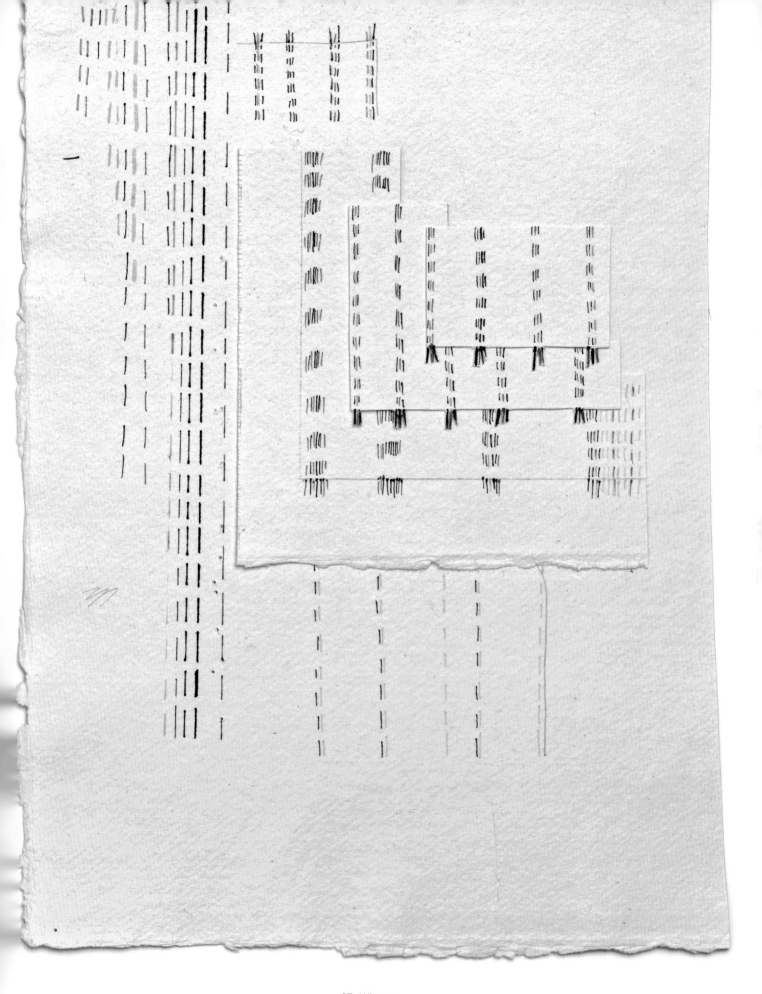

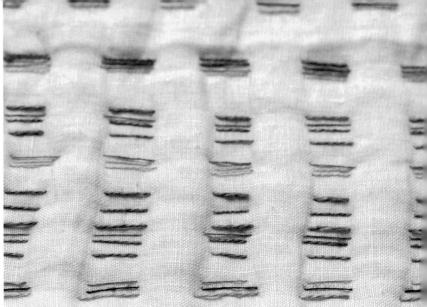

Exploring winter cold and warmth

Woven, layered and felted textiles have been used to provide warmth in different cultures for many centuries. For this textile piece I wanted to combine the real physical warmth and emotional comfort of a bed quilt with some of my photographs and ideas about winter cold. I decided to make a simple functional bed quilt of recycled fabrics, linen threads and a vintage blanket from my stock. The paperwork used to develop this simple quilt is minimal, as shown on page 97.

The resulting quilt, called *Comfort Blanket*, has a top layer of lightly textured bright white cotton sheet, the centre is a reused traditional cream 'Witney' type wool blanket and the backing fabric is another repurposed sheet, this time in a duller white. The threads are a mixture of linen weaving threads and vintage linen threads, chosen for their matt finish and strength. The threads needed to be strong to withstand being pulled through the fabric many times as I stitched the whole length of the quilt with one length of thread for each line. Sometimes I waxed the threads to avoid breakage and reduce wear. I used quite large parallel running stitches, placed in groups. The quilt is finished simply with turned edges on all sides and knots at the two long edges.

My use of running stitch is partly because I still love the simple, calming and meditative process of stitching it and partly a nod to the textiles of other times and cultures that have inspired me. These techniques, including *kantha*, *sashiko* and *boro* (see opposite) were used to extend the life of precious worn fabric pieces by layering and stitching. My reuse of sheets and a vintage blanket in this quilt echoes this approach.

Making a simple seasonally inspired quilt, blending and integrating many of the ideas and approaches in this book into one complete whole seems a suitable end point for the four seasonal chapters of this book.

Above left and right: Details of hand stitching on *Comfort Blanket*

Right: *Comfort Blanket* bed quilt

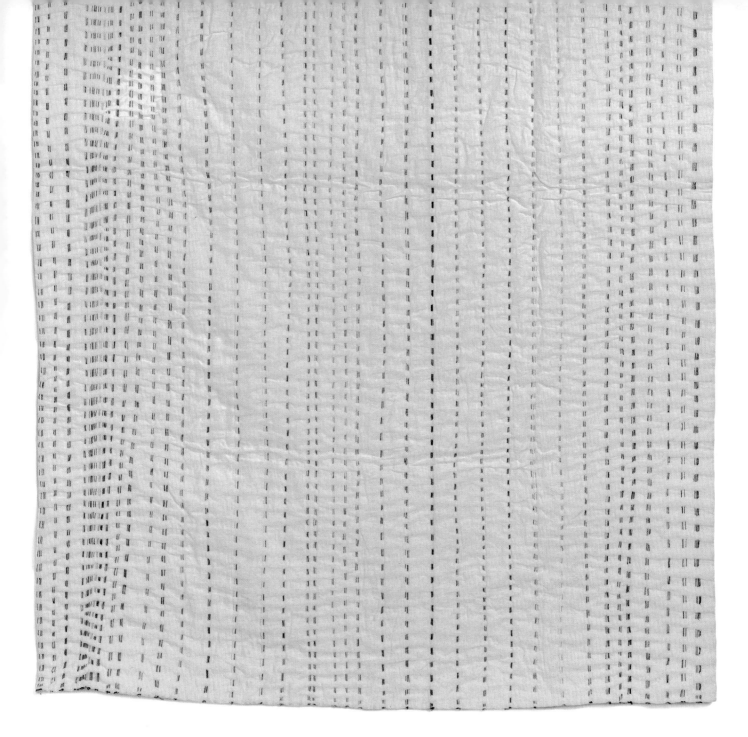

SOME TRADITIONAL LAYERING & STITCHING TECHNIQUES

Sashiko: Sashiko is a traditional Japanese technique using small, carefully placed running stitches on layered used and worn fabrics to create beautiful decorative patterns and to strengthen the precious fabrics and prolong their life. Traditionally worked in white cotton thread on blue indigo dyed fabrics.

Boro: Boro are old layered, mended or patched textiles originating in northern Japan. A boro item of clothing or furnishing would be patched and stitched again and again as it was handed down over generations.

Kantha: Kantha embroidery uses old saris layered together, hand stitched in parallel lines of running stitch, to create a soft, light, somewhat rippled textile.

CHAPTER 5

Ways of working

Walking locally throughout the year, observing and recording
the passing seasons using photographs, is the basis of this book.
My walks are a source of visual and sensory inspiration and
experience, as well as opportunities for thought and reflection.
The previous chapters explored ideas, images and techniques
related to ten of the seasonal aspects seen on my walks. All these
ideas and techniques could contribute to developing your creative
vocabulary to express your own ideas through seasonally inspired
textile work.

Some ideas, inspirations and techniques occur more than once,
used in different ways at different seasonal moments. Other ideas
and techniques occur just once, as they seemed to fit best with one
specific season or one aspect of a season.

Detail of old rope on a
gatepost after heavy rain

A seasonal year

There are many other ways that the changing seasons could influence your creative life. It could be fascinating to choose a subject and follow it throughout the year. Possible subjects include views observed from the same vantage point each time or an individual tree, wall or plant. Establishing a regular pattern of walking and observing throughout the year would enable you to take photographs of your chosen subject during the four main seasons, or maybe every month, and use them for inspiration. Perhaps you could experiment with daily walks and taking photographs for a year or part of a year.

Sustained engagement with a single subject over time can pay great dividends. Artist Carolyn Curtis Magri used drone footage of moorland taken during the course of one day as a starting point to develop a series of images using watercolour and digital manipulation over the subsequent months. Some of her images are shown here.

Below left: Watercolour and digital images, Carolyn Curtis Magri

Below right: Detail of iPhone image, Carolyn Curtis Magri

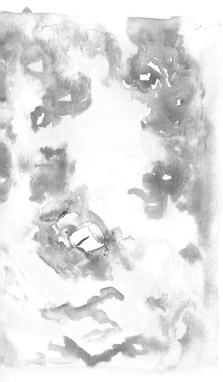

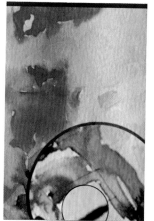
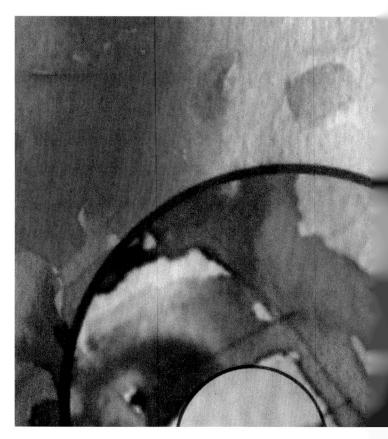

Making & using stitched samples

As you will have seen throughout this book, making samples is a fundamental part of my textile practice in all seasons. My samples provide many functions and benefits: recording inspiration and new ideas; experimenting with techniques; developing finished textile works and the simple enjoyment of stitching.

Recording inspiration and new ideas

The first type of sample I make is one related to something new I have observed in passing and found inspiring: maybe the shape or pattern attracts me or sparks an idea for a stitched mark. Such a one-off sample is often quickly made and somewhat sketchy. I aim to record the idea in stitch before I lose it. The sample is successful if it reminds me strongly of what I have seen. The sample shown was made after walking around the walled gardens at West Dean College in West Sussex before a day of teaching. There was something exciting and special in the form and shape of the fuschia-flowering gooseberry shown in the photograph.

Below left: Branches of a flowering gooseberry, West Dean walled gardens

Below right: One-off sample based on my memory of what I had seen

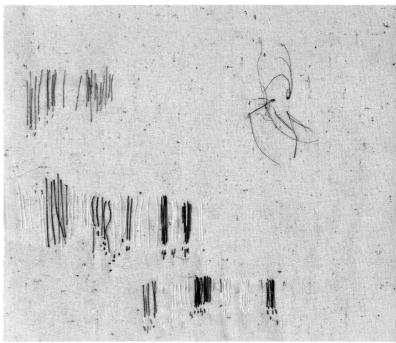

Exploring a technique

The second type of sample is a structured and methodical exploration of a technique made from a range of fabrics and types of stitching. The detail shown left is from a sample made to explore 16 variations on corded quilting (the full sample set is illustrated on pages 84 and 85). Inspired by the vertical ribs of bleached plant stems, parts of the sample are stitched by hand, parts by machine. The results vary in how successfully they reflect the original visual source material. However, this exploratory sample does offer lots of potential for future work.

Developing a finished textile work

The third type of sample is the one I create as I develop my ideas towards a completed textile artwork. I use samples to explore which materials and techniques will be the most suitable to express my idea. I begin with my general creative direction clear in my mind, usually partly worked through in some paper-based sketches, and then I make many small samples. I use different fabric, stitch and thread combinations with a stitch technique, or techniques, to more fully develop my idea. Each sample made takes me closer to the finished textile artwork, as illustrated in the sequence of samples shown here.

Above: Detail of corded sample

Right: Paperwork for *Spring/Summer Yellow/ Green Radiant*

Worked example using development samples

I began with a simple photocopied drawing and the early decision to use a dark green cotton sateen fabric and hand-stitched radiant shapes using bold threads worked in a grid across the whole surface (see Chapter 1 for more on radiant stitch).

I made a series of samples as I developed the idea further. A lightweight polyester wadding gave a softly raised finish to the central circular shape. The raised effect came solely from the choice of materials and the placement of the stitches; no additional padding was needed. The first sample (top right) was based on a square grid with the radiating marks stitched in cream and mid-green threads. The next sample was based on a diagonal grid, while the third sample retained the diagonal grid and included more threads in greens and yellows with some sky blue. After making the second sample, I noticed that the diagonal grid gave a more energetic spring/summer feel to the piece than the square grid. Adding stitches in sky blue threads to the last sample better reflected the sky and made the effect livelier. This ensured that the finished piece more closely expressed what I had seen and experienced. The final work, *Spring/Summer Yellow/Green Radiant*, (detail below), has two diagonal crossed lines of radiating marks in which yellows dominate.

Right: Development samples
for *Spring/Summer Yellow/
Green Radiant*

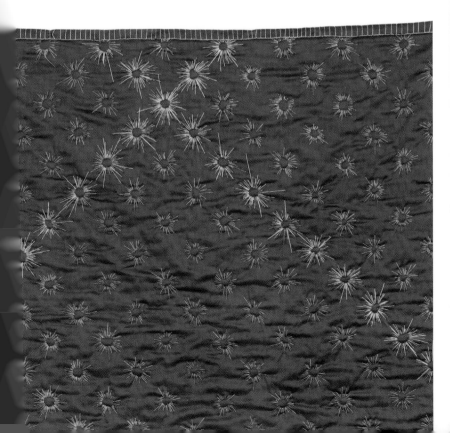

Collections of samples

Over time, one-off samples build up into a group of ideas and jottings, mostly worked on small oddments of fabric that were 'hanging around' my studio and came to hand easily. The colours can be a bit random at times, as it is often a texture or a feeling that I'm seeking to capture, rather than an accurate memory of colours. Capturing these tiny moments of inspiration in this way means I am relaxed knowing that these ideas are available if I need to refer to them at some point in the future. The sample of detached chain stitch shown on page 59 was made in 2011 and some years later it inspired my chain-stitched midsummer trees.

One way of giving these one-off samples more substance is to spread them out, grouping and placing them carefully in relation to each other, then photographing the layout. Photographs such as this record and date the samples and enable me to refer to them more easily. I rarely keep my paper notebooks for more than a few years, sometimes much less, yet my stitched sample pieces, however tiny, are almost never discarded. They are simply too important to me to let them go. These samples may never lead directly to a full-scale piece of textile work as there are just too many ideas and not enough hours and days. However, these samples are a vital record and a source of satisfaction.

Above: Group of one-off samples with potential for further development

Right: Cactus, Fuerteventura

Being away from home

A change of scene is welcome and often creatively inspiring at any time of year. For many of us, summer brings the opportunity of some time away and a chance to relax and explore new places and maybe spend more time outside. Visits and holidays can also be an opportunity to enjoy activities that daily life rarely allows enough time for – maybe a little sketching or people watching.

Many of us will recall going to the beach during the school holidays with particular pleasure. As adults we are often still drawn to the coastline and its beauty, variety and changeability have much to offer textile artists. Refer to my earlier book, *Mark-Making in Textile Art*, which looks in some detail at hand stitch and beaches and includes illustrations of textile pieces inspired by shifting sands and tide lines.

Walking is a key holiday activity for me, focused on seeing, exploring and taking photographs of my new surroundings. It is an opportunity to practise seeing and observing new places and cultures without seeking a specific result. While away, if you are so minded, you could practise observing your new surroundings and aim to create a resource of inspiring photographs for you to draw on when you are back at home.

Holiday walks

If you want to use your visits and holidays to further your creative textile work, here are some suggestions based on themed walks. You could choose one theme each day, or consider a single theme for a few days.

Walk 1: First impressions

Set out to explore your new surroundings and notice what catches your eye first. Take some photos of your first impressions. The example above right shows a first-impression photograph taken in Crete.

Observe, too, what really excites you. Is it the architecture, aspects of the landscape, symbols and colours used by another culture, the churches or religious buildings, the written script used by the locals, the light, the climate? One aspect, or many aspects?

When you pause later that day to review your photographs and experiences do you notice any recurrent themes? What most excites you creatively? Then select a new theme for the following day's walk.

Walk 2: Exploring new places

You may find that you go out for a walk with your chosen theme in mind and you return inspired by something quite different. That's fine: sometimes life and exploring are like that. Coastal and beach walks are often very special because of the frequently changing interactions of the light, the tides and the land. Occasionally, you may catch an unusual storm or light effect as shown above, far right, where a summer thunderstorm provided an opportunity to take some beautiful, unexpected and intensely colourful photographs. What I was seeing was so much more exciting than my original theme for the day and opened up new colour ideas for subsequent textile work. These photographs particularly influenced my colour choices for the textile work *Nine Yards or Thereabouts*.

Above: Cretan view

Above right: Summer storm at Flamborough, Yorkshire

More suggested themes for holiday beach walks

Colour
Set out to observe as many colours as possible, or alternatively look for only one colour, say green or white, on a single walk. Or look only for high contrasts such as black and white, or opposites on the colour wheel such as blue and orange.

Shells, pebbles, coral, fossils
Try looking for a single type, colour, marking, pattern or size of your chosen object each day.

Stripes/bands
How many distinct types of stripes and bands can you see? Look at different scales, such as large stripes on cliff faces and tiny stripes found on shells. What can you find that surprises you? Perhaps the colour combinations are amazing, subtle or jarring? Look at where the sea meets the land; what kind of stripe or band is this?

Patterns
Look for animal and bird tracks or patterns of bird movement in the sky.

Textures
How many different textures can you find? Beaches at low tide may have lots of sand ripples, worm casts, seaweeds and much more variety of texture than you might expect. Muddy, often estuarine, beaches seem to be especially richly textured. Notice, too, when the textures underfoot change. Large expanses of beach can vary widely in the feel of the sand or mud beneath your feet. Your return walk may be very different to the outward one. Be aware of the real risk to safety at the coast including incoming tides and cliff edges. Beaches can have quicksands and tidal marshes, which

should be avoided. Be aware, too, that you are likely to be on unfamiliar territory and walk only where you are quite sure it is safe to do so.

Processes

What natural processes can you observe? Look for changing tides, streams and pools. Look for fleeting changes as well as the more obvious shifts of the tide and wind. Consider the differences between a beach in summer and in winter.

Human activity at the coast

If the visual aspects of human activity interest you, experiment with some of these themes for your walks.

People

Observe people on the beach who may be in groups, pairs or walking alone. Notice their sizes, ages, groupings and position in the wider landscape. People play games, put up tents, windsurf, walk their dogs and do much more on beaches. Their varied activities can create interesting shapes and movements to photograph.

Colour

People bring objects with them onto beaches: vividly coloured windbreaks, kites, surf boards, balls, buckets and spades can provide new and unexpected juxtapositions and combinations of colours for the keen observer. People's clothing can be a rich source of inspiration when seen against the background of sky, sea and sand. Small children, especially, are often wearing striking colour combinations.

Machines

Look at fairground rides and other coastal machinery. Seen out of season they can look very different, often sad, in comparison to how they look in use during the summer season.

Harbours

Look at harbours, moorings and other items associated with fishing and leisure sailing such as boats, rigging, flags, nets, crates and lobster pots. Many of these items are stitched in some way.

Maritime buildings

Specialized maritime buildings often look different to those found inland, with very particular functions and shapes. Military and coastal fortifications, lighthouses, groynes, houses, seaside cafés and beach huts are all worth looking at closely. Consider their purpose and how their structures reflect that intention. Are the materials used in their construction old or new, local or imported? Observe any weathering due to exposure to sunlight, wind or salt water.

Above left: Beach view

Above: Lacing on a sailing boat

Text

Text can be found in many coastal places, on signs, on structures such as sea defences and boats, written in the sand or on fragments of paper. Such text is often weathered, worn and faded, adding to its visual interest and appeal.

Pattern and textures

Created by many types of human activity, patterns and textures are everywhere; stacks of deckchairs, displays of beach toys, railings along a promenade, house doors, the tyre tracks of lifeguards' vehicles across the sand, boats grouped in a harbour seen from a cliff above, and so on.

Beyond the coast

Many of these suggested themes can also be observed and photographed for inspiration on urban or rural visits. Choose whichever suggestions from the list above resonate with you and your surroundings. Reflections in water or glass are worth looking for, wherever you are. Often temporary phenomena, when the light or breeze changes they disappear. Interesting examples include the sky reflected in tidal pools or puddles, trees mirrored in a still river or pond and the peachy light of sunrise or sunset reflected in glazed city buildings. What else can you see?

Collecting

Collect small holiday souvenirs such as tickets and packaging, postcards, shells and pebbles and so on. Be sure to collect shells, discarded fishing line and other beach items only where it is safe and legal to do so.

Back at home

Reviewing

When you get home, take stock of the photographs you have, any sketches and notes you have made and any souvenirs you have collected. Ensure you have your digital photographs safely backed up. You may wish to print out some of your photographs to have as a physical reference, instead of looking at them on screen. Once you have gathered everything together, settle yourself down to have a good look at what you have observed and photographed. Are there any recurrent themes? Maybe a particular building or pattern recurs, or maybe it is a repeated group of colours you find pleasing and which is typical of a different climate or culture? Sometimes the processes of taking stock, sorting and filing are necessary to find out and start to get to grips with what it is that really excited you creatively. At other times one theme or subject may immediately stand out.

Once you have found two or three of these recurrent themes or subjects, make a note of them, pause and see which of them is the most important for you to explore further at this point. Which theme or subject has the most energy and attraction? Do you know why? For further clarification you may wish to look back at digital and other images you have collected during visits and holidays: does this theme or subject occur there too? Are your choices and interests consistent over time or have they changed?

Keeping it all safe

I find it useful to have both a physical file/box and an online folder of digital photographs. I file my digital photographs grouped by date and event using my computer's software. I also have a range of online folders of digital photographs on themes I am interested in such as plant forms or allover textures. Copying your digital photographs to the relevant online folders keeps them easily available to refer to as needed. I find having both real and virtual places to put related images and objects keeps my mind and my studio clear, which helps me both to focus and find space to work.

Seeing with fresh eyes

For a few days after you get back from being away you are likely to see your home and your locality with fresh eyes. This can be a really rewarding time to walk around your neighbourhood and observe it anew. This effect usually lasts for a few days and can be helpful in clarifying what exactly it is in your locality that really interests you. You may also notice that the seasonal timing at home is earlier, later or entirely different to the place you have just visited.

A note on more distant and different cultures

Many of us now have the opportunity to travel further afield and more often to places that are very different to our home locality, whether for holidays or work. The opportunity to see and experience a different culture can be creatively very significant, with lasting effects on your understanding of the world, which can, over time, have important impacts on your textile art and life. You may, for example, notice symbols and ideas that occur and connect different cultures and places. My interest in the Tree of Life symbol has been deepened by finding the idea expressed in and shared by other cultures across space and time.

When I visited Japan in the 1990s I was unable to speak or write the language so I could not understand the signage on the buildings and roads. I relied heavily on my visual skills to make sense of my surroundings, which made for an intense few weeks. What I saw, felt and experienced on that visit permanently changed my understanding of materials, how they can be used and how a maker's knowledge of a material develops over time, often over very long periods of time. On my return I saw my own country and locality in new ways. Derbyshire and England appeared to be especially green and the history distinct and special.

These experiences of a very different culture took a few years to permeate through and influence my textile work. Hindsight and photographs are both helpful in tracing these influences. The photos I took on my Japanese visit were taken and printed using film and earlier technologies, so they are inevitably somewhat faded now, yet they still remind me powerfully of other ways of living, seeing and making.

Group of photographs
from my visit to Japan

Being inspired by history and archives

I have always been interested in history/prehistory, subjects composed of many seasons and different periods. My route into making stitched textiles was through seeing exhibitions of traditional 19th- and 20th-century North Country whole cloth quilts, red and green appliqué quilts and Amish quilts pieced from dark, solid-coloured fabrics. These quilted textiles embody particular social, economic and historical contexts, just as textile work made now embodies the circumstances of our own time.

In 2014 I was invited to participate in an exhibition project with Bradford College's Textile Archive. I welcomed the opportunity to get really close to their wonderful collection of early dye sample books, pattern books, journals and workbooks of former students, often presented in one-off, handmade folders and quirky formats with fascinating bindings. Gathered and donated from many sources and containing many smaller archives, the collection is a unique record of the role of textiles, especially wool, in the development of Bradford, its landscapes and people, and of the evolution of the technologies of dyeing and textile manufacture.

After much deliberation I chose to work with the notebook of Mary Ware, an innovative 18th-century 'callico printer' working in partnership with her husband in Crayford, Kent, near London. In the 1760s the Wares developed a unique copperplate printing technique known as 'double strike'. More properly called an order book, the loosely stitched pages of Mary Ware's notebook recorded the details and costs of various copperplate printing work carried out for named clients.

As well as the names of the clients and their orders, the notebook contains hundreds of hand-drawn designs for textile prints. A printer called Vint was active in the 1780s and probably took over the assets of the Wares some time after the widowed Mary went bankrupt in 1782. The designs were, most probably, created for a later textile printing firm trading as Vint and Gilling. Their partnership was active between 1792 and 1802. Vint and Gilling probably reused the pages of the order book by turning it upside down. Paper was an expensive and precious material in the 18th century and this kind of reuse was common.

The image, right, shows
a double page from Mary
Ware's order book, with the
handwritten order for 'Fancy
Plate Handkerchiefs' for a client called J. Hignell, on the right-
hand side. On the left-hand page the writing is hidden by the paper
print designs pasted on top. The print designs were then numbered
300 to 309.

Within these textile designs I found a plant-based Tree of Life
design numbered 255, which I have adapted and used several
times since. The long, thin format of my exhibition piece for
Bradford Textile Archive was influenced by the blue bundle of
weaving diagrams shown in the general view above. This bundle is
a collection of working diagrams, the pages taped together by their
short edges and is several yards/metres long when fully unrolled.

In my supporting research into 18th-century textile history I
discovered that a line of blue thread was woven into the selvedge
of fabrics produced in Britain at this time. I have reused this idea
in the line of blue hand stitch seen in part of the *Nine Yards or
Thereabouts* textile and I used it again on one edge of my *Comfort
Blanket* quilt shown in the Winter chapter on page 99. The title
Nine Yards or Thereabouts was inspired by a notice in the Public
Advertiser of 18 February 1775, which offered a reward for a length
of stolen printed calico with Mary Ware's name and described as
'nine yards or thereabouts' in length.

Carrying out an annual review

I find it helpful to review and reflect on the work I have made each year and consider my creative direction. Ensuring I create time for an annual review and reflection is important in keeping my work developing and my excitement levels high. Excitement is important to prioritizing creative work over other enjoyable (and less enjoyable) activities. It really helps to find the right time to do this within the rhythm of the seasons and your own life and circumstances. For many years this review process was part of my creative activities at New Year. More recently I have come to appreciate that it suits me better to do an annual review in September when I come back to the studio after the summer with new ideas and fresh energy.

I consider how I have progressed with the theme and projects I have been working on during the year. What worked and what was less successful? Do I want to continue with my current theme or change it? What creative activities does the year ahead hold and have I allowed enough time for making new work, seeing exhibitions and studio time?

Then I consider the three words: STOP, START, CONTINUE – what I can stop doing, start doing and continue to do to move my work forward. I make a list of activities below each word to help me think about options.

I usually consider which of my themes recur year after year. Long-standing themes of mine are working with layers of whole cloth (not pieced) fabrics, hand stitching, landscape and history. Other themes come and go as exhibitions and projects develop and are completed. A theme may drop away only to reappear some years later.

I will often write notes and pages of longhand text to help with this review process. The process of writing itself is usually clarifying and sometimes revelatory. As the expression says, it can be effective to 'sleep on it'. I do this by reviewing my notes and images in the evening, sleeping and then writing down my thoughts in longhand first thing in the morning. Sometimes this approach yields significant insights, ideas and synergies.

Finishing and displaying textile artworks

The finished textile artworks illustrated in this book are made using several approaches and formats reflecting the different origin, purpose and content of each example. I have included some wall-hung pieces such as *Spring/Summer Yellow/Green Radiant* (page 45) and *Stellate Meadow* (page 57). On these pieces I have added a sleeve for a wooden batten at the top on the reverse side. The wooden batten is thin enough to ensure that the finished work hangs flat to the wall. Traditional North Country whole cloth quilts inspired the functional quilt *Comfort Blanket* on page 99, which is simply finished with hand-stitched edges and hand-tied knots. Some of the smaller pieces shown are stitched and then mounted over a shaped wooden stretcher. Examples include *Red is the First Colour of Spring,* the two *Equinox* panels (in the Spring chapter, on page 42 and 43) and the *Sun Wheel* panel at the end of the Summer chapter – see page 69.

The *Nine Yards or Thereabouts* exhibition piece (shown on pages 114–115) is 23 x 820cm (9 x 320in). For ease of working, it was made in small sections, which were then joined into four longer pieces. These four sections were then joined into two pairs and then finally joined together into one very long quilt. This long, thin format was chosen to echo the unusual formats found in the Bradford Textile Archive. The finished work is intended to be displayed hung high up on a wall, flowing down onto a low plinth along the floor.

When making a series of works it can be helpful for them to have a standard format. It is easier to work this way and repeated use of a format improves the final results. Additionally, the final group of works is likely to appear more coherent when displayed. The recent vogue for journal quilts, made to a set size and shape over the course of a year is a successful example of this approach. Discipline and time-based structures such as making journal quilts for exhibition deadlines can be helpful.

And finally

I do hope that you have enjoyed this book and found much of interest and inspiration in the contents, and that you will return to it for reference in the future. I hope that you will look at your own locality with new eyes, greater appreciation and understanding and approach your time away from home differently too. The world has much beauty and inspiration to offer us. We are fortunate to have time and resources to explore it. I trust that you will go on to make very personal and distinctive stitched textile works as you explore being inspired by the seasons in your own locality.

Detail of tags
and stitches

CHAPTER 6

Equipment and materials

Making personal textile work can involve many processes and a range of equipment and materials. Very little equipment is needed when you get started on making textile art, and you can add to and upgrade your equipment over time as the opportunity arises and your preferences evolve. My preference is to have versatile, simple equipment and to work with materials that are easy and pleasurable to use.

The sampling process covered in Chapter 5 is fundamental to finding suitable combinations of equipment, materials and techniques that express your ideas and really suit you personally. As you make these choices over time and get to understand your equipment, materials and techniques ever more deeply, your work will develop a more distinctive, personal nature and you will probably enjoy making even more.

Equipment and materials

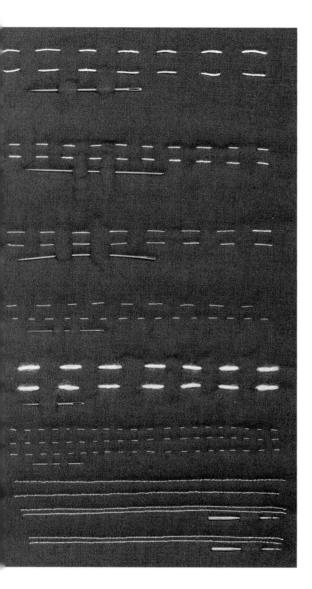

Selection of different sizes of hand and machine sewing needles. The stitching shown uses appropriate threads for each size of needle.

Equipment

The lists of equipment below are given in the same order as the making process, beginning with photography and ending with sewing.

Working with photography and computers

- Digital camera on your mobile phone and, later, a digital SLR camera.
- Colour printer/scanner/ photocopier or access to one; paper for printing photographs.
- Computer and software for reviewing and storing digital photographs.
- Specialist software if you wish to manipulate your digital images.

Working with art media

- A range of brushes and other means of applying paint in a wide range of sizes and types, for example foam brushes for laying down large areas of colour, smaller household decorating brushes and small artists' brushes for detailed work.
- A range of other means of applying paint: spatulas, repurposed plastic credit cards, potters' tools, sponges, feathers, twigs and dried stems.

Measuring and cutting

- Various rulers: a 30cm (12in) plastic ruler to begin with and later a metal metre rule; a couple of specialist gridded quilting rulers can be very useful too.

- A cloth tape measure and a lockable metal retractable tape measure.
- Scissors, ideally several pairs for different functions. My range of scissors includes a sharp pair used only for cutting fabrics and other scissors for cutting paper, plastics and card. I buy the same type and size of scissors each time.
- A small pair of pointed scissors for fine work.
- Specialist scissors such as appliqué scissors and pinking shears are sometimes useful and can be collected over time.
- Craft knife or scalpel with spare blades.
- Self-healing cutting mats: having a range of different sizes suited to your working space is helpful.
- An awl or stiletto for punching holes.

Marking

The items listed below are alternatives. Different projects will need different types or colours of marker. Experimentation is helpful before you commit yourself to a method of marking on a particular fabric.

- Washable marker pen, usually blue, is probably the most versatile option.
- Watercolour pencils in colours to contrast with the surface being marked.
- Pencil with a fine hard lead.
- Dressmakers' chalk.

Sewing

- Long glass-headed pins, flower pins and curved quilting safety pins.
- Needles: Japanese sashiko, long darners, sharps, tiny traditional hand-quilting needles.
- Sewing machine suitable for free machining, with manufacturers' instruction book.
- A range of machine sewing needles appropriate for your machine.
- Block of beeswax for smoothing and strengthening rough or fluffy threads for hand stitching.
- Steam iron and an adjustable-height ironing board.
- A stitch ripper can be useful at times.

The size of needle you use is important in several ways. It is worth experimenting with a wide range of needles to find what sizes and types suit your purpose and sewing machine or your hands. Hand stitching layers of fabric is easiest with a longer needle as it is more flexible as you manipulate the fabric layers. I mostly use larger sizes of long darner needles and imported Japanese sashiko needles.

It is fun to experiment with new equipment and materials, adding new tools based on recommendations from friends and magazine reviews or finds from vintage fairs and charity shops. Tagging guns came onto the market some years after I had started making quilts and it took me a while to take the risk and try one. I now use my tagging gun a great deal for holding the fabrics together as I make samples and would not be without it. I occasionally incorporate the tags themselves into my finished work (see the image on page 118 at the start of this chapter).

Other useful items

- Sticky tape, masking tape.
- Staple gun (manual or electric) for mounting work on wooden stretchers or frames.
- Tagging gun and tags in black and white.
- Recycled plastic containers or packaging, brown and coloured wrapping papers, envelopes, light card, plastics and corrugated cardboard.

Above: Selection of waddings: From right to left: bonded polyester, cotton, needle-punched wool felt, acrylic felt, old cream wool 'Witney' blanket, lightweight polyester wadding.

Materials

For paperworks and design

- Papers: heavyweight lining paper (sold for wallpapering), tissue, tracing, cartridge, graph and squared papers. Layout paper for working on designs. Textured watercolour papers and papers for printing out photographs.

- Pencils/crayons: wax crayons, candles, chinagraph pencils (a white chinagraph pencil is the most useful, but other colours are also available), watercolour pencils and graphite pencils in a range of hardnesses, oil pastels, water-soluble crayons, e.g. Neocolor.
- Pens/inks: felt pens of many sizes and types, biros, ink pen and a range of nibs.
- Paints: watercolours, Brusho, ready-mixed poster paints, acrylics and household emulsion paints.
- Glue: a glue stick for light work and PVA glue for thicker or heavier work.
- Sticky tape and masking tape in different widths.

For stitching

The idea of simplicity is important to me so I keep a stock of neutral fabrics and threads that I can colour to suit my purpose. Choosing a good combination of fabrics, thread types and thicknesses for the stitch techniques you plan to use is fundamental to the look of your finished textile art work and how easy and enjoyable the work will be to complete. This is especially relevant for larger textile works, which will take many hours to complete.

Fabrics

I prefer to use fabrics made from natural fibres. I collect discarded clothes in natural fabrics for their softness and character. Cotton fibre, for example, can be woven and treated in many ways to give a wide range of fabric and thread types as seen in the examples. I mostly stitch on three layers of a cotton fabric, often using a well-washed calico for all the layers, to create enough stability to support the weight of my stitching. Avoid hard or stiff fabrics, especially when stitching by hand.

I also enjoy using fabrics that have meaning for me. I have made samples and art textiles from fabrics given to me by friends, used threads purchased on holiday and used vintage fabrics from my family. When I look back at the textile works I have made over the years, they record who I have known and where I have travelled, adding to my enjoyment.

Fabrics list

- Natural-fibre fabrics: cotton, silk, linen and wool including calico, muslin and mixtures.
- New and repurposed fabrics in natural fibres including

cotton sheeting, calico, silk and linen.
- Bondaweb or iron-on Vilene to stabilize the back of stitched work

Wadding/batting

Sometimes I use cotton fabrics for the top and bottom layers of a piece, with a suitable wadding sandwiched between them. The waddings I use regularly include polyester for its lightness and loft, cotton for weight and stability, and vintage cream wool 'Witney' blankets for their greater weight and a more solid final result.

Waddings list

- 2oz polyester wadding, cotton wadding, vintage woollen blankets.

Threads

Stitched marks are an important part of my textile work. I enjoy the way the same technique can look very different stitched using threads of varying thicknesses, colours and types. I seek to understand the potential of the stitch and the most suitable fabrics and threads with which to work.

Hand stitching offers more choices for exploring different thicknesses and types of thread than machine stitching does. When sewing by machine, the thread thickness has to pass through the eye of the machine's needle. Using thicker threads in the bobbin

of a machine can provide some interesting possibilities. See the bibliography on page 124 for further ideas.

Threads list

- Machine and hand sewing threads, embroidery and flower threads, crochet threads in a range of thicknesses and fibres including cotton, linen, silk, rayon and wool.
- Specialist quilting threads.

For colouring fabrics and threads

- Fibre-reactive dyes such as Dylon, fabric pens and silk paints.

Below: Examples of neutral fabrics and threads. From front to back: velvet, muslin, sateen curtain lining, calico and washed heavy calico.

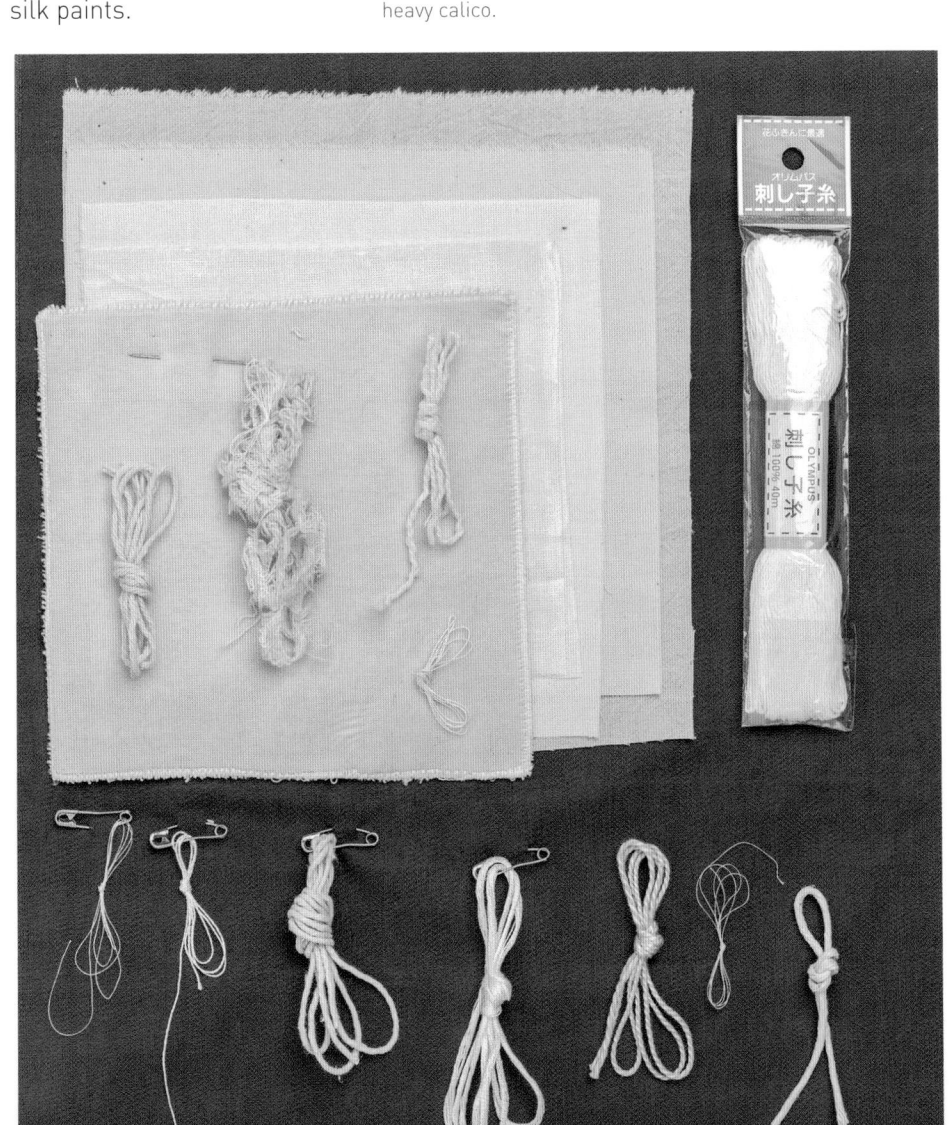

Resources

Bibliography

Blossfeldt, Karl, *Art Forms in the Plant World*. Dover, USA (1985)

Briscoe, Susan, *The Ultimate Sashiko Sourcebook* (2005)

Broun, Sheila, *Listen to the Earth*. Exhibition Catalogue, Leeds, UK (1990)

Browne, Clare, Davies, Glyn and Micheal, M.A.(eds), *English Medieval Embroidery: Opus Anglicanum*. Yale/Victoria and Albert Museum (2016)

Butler, Anne, *The Batsford Encyclopaedia of Embroidery Stitches*. Batsford (1983)

Campbell-Harding, Val and Watts, Pamela, *Machine Embroidery Stitch Techniques*. Batsford (1989)

Chapman, S.D. and Chassagne, S., *European Textile Printers in the Eighteenth Century*. Heinemann (1981)

Cane, Kyra, *Making and Drawing*. Bloomsbury (2012)

Carey, Frances, *The Tree Meaning and Myth*. The British Museum Press (2012)

Davidson, George (ed.), *Roget's Thesaurus*. Penguin (2002)

Eaton, Linda, *Printed Textiles: British and American cottons and linens 1700–1850*. The Monacelli Press, USA (2014)

Eddy, Celia, *Quilted Planet: A sourcebook of quilts from around the world*. Mitchell Beasley (2005)

Ford, T.D. and Rieuwerts, J.H. (eds), *Lead Mining in the Peak District*. Landmark Publishing (2000)

Frost, Shirley, *Whirlow: The story of an ancient Sheffield hamlet*. J.W. Northend Ltd, Sheffield (1990)

Hiebert, Frederik and Cambon, P., *Afghanistan: crossroads of the Ancient World*. The British Museum Press (2011)

Hill, Paul, *White Peak, Dark Peak*. Cornerhouse Publications, Manchester (1990)

Hoskins, W.G., *The Making of the English Landscape*. Hodder & Stoughton (1995, revised 1988)

Macfarlane, Robert, *Landmarks*. Hamish Hamilton (2015)

Marsh, Gail, *Eighteenth-century Embroidery Techniques*. Guild of Master Craftsman Publications (2006)

Moss, Gillian, 'British Copperplate Printed Textiles', *Antiques* magazine. April, USA (1990)

Parrott, Helen, *Mark-making in Textile Art*. Batsford (2013)

Osler, Dorothy, *Traditional British Quilts*. Batsford (1987)

Quilters Guild *Quilt Treasures*. Deirdre Macdonald Books. Anne Macdonald Books (1995/ 2010 reissue)

Rackham, Oliver, *The History of the Countryside*. Phoenix Press, London (1986)

Renouf, Eloise, *20 Ways to Draw a Tree and 44 Other Nifty Things from Nature*. Quarry Books, USA (2013)

Robinson, Tim, *Connemara: the last pool of darkness*. Penguin, Ireland (2008)

Shepherd, Nan, *The Living Mountain*. Canongate Books, Edinburgh (2011)

Skelton, R., *Beyond the Fell Wall*. Little Toller Books, Dorset (2015)

Smibert, Tony and Townsend, Joyce, *Tate Watercolour Manual*. Tate Publishing (2014)

Smith, Roly, *A Peak District Anthology*. Frances Lincoln Ltd (2012)

Sykas, Philip Anthony, *The Secret Life of Textiles: six pattern book archives in North West England*. Bolton Museums and Art Gallery (2005)

Tharp, Twyla, *The Creative Habit: learn it and use it for life*. Simon & Schuster, New York (2003)

Tinkler, Nikki, *Handbook of Quilting and Patchwork Stitches*. Search Press (2011)

Turnbull, G., *A History of the Calico Printing Industry in Great Britain*. John Sherratt & Son (1951)

Tsuzuki, Kyoichi , *Boro: Rags and Tatters from the Far North of Japan*. Aspect Corp (2009)

Uglow, Jenny, *Nature's Engraver: a life of Thomas Bewick*. Faber & Faber Ltd (2006)

White, Gilbert, *Gilbert White's Year*. Oxford University Press. (1982)

Winchester, Angus J.L., *Dry Stone Walls*. Amberley Publishing, Stroud, Gloucestershire, UK (2016)

Zaman, Niaz, *The Art of Kantha Embroidery*. University Press Ltd, Bangladesh (2014)

Magazines

Specialist magazines can provide useful current information and inspiration beyond the world of textiles. Some suggestions are:

Embroidery www.mymagazinesub.co.uk/embroidery/
Selvedge www.selvedge.org
The Quilter www.quiltersguild.org.uk/membership/the-quilter
Ceramic Review www.ceramicreview.com/magazine/
Crafts www.craftscouncil.org.uk/magazine/issues
Printmaking Today www.cellopress.co.uk/page/printmaking-today

Websites

AN formerly Artists Newsletter www.a-n.co.uk
AXIS www.axisweb.org
Bradford College Textile Archive www.bradfordcollege.ac.uk/about/arts-culture/textile-archive
Crayford Mary Ware ran her calico printing business in Crayford, Kent, England. http://swaislands.crayfordhistory.co.uk/library/The%20Fabric%20of%20Our%20Town%20Education%20booklet%20MAIN%20STORY.pdf
Glenthorne Quaker Centre and Guest House, Grasmere, Cumbria www.glenthorne.org.uk
Helen Parrott www.helenparrott.co.uk
Instagram: @landandlight
Peak District Mines Historical Society www.pdmhs.com
Quilters Guild including the British Quilt Study Group www.quiltersguild.org.uk

Suppliers

Art Van Go /www.vycombe-arts.co.uk/onlineshop/
Colourcraft www.colourcraftltd.com
Fred Aldous shops in Manchester and Leeds or online www.fredaldous.co.uk
John Lewis stores nationwide: www.johnlewis.com
The Patchwork Garden shop in Sheffield and online www.thepatchworkgarden.co.uk
Quiltessential shop at Cromford Mill, Derbyshire or www.quiltessential.co.uk
Whaleys www.whaleys-bradford.ltd.uk
Vintage and antique fairs and charity shops for textile books, needles and interesting vintage threads
Textile and craft events including the annual Knitting and Stitching shows and the annual Festival of Quilts.

Some of the tracks and traces of people to be found in my locality

Settlement: hamlet, village, town, houses/huts, city, mills, schools, churches/chapels, labs, gardens

Ownership and access: enclosures, fences and gates, walls, signposts and signage

Agriculture: grazing, fields, hay making, meadows, growing and harvesting crops, allotments

Power: water mills, leats and dams, power cables

Transport: paths, tracks, rivers, turnpike roads, canals, railways, motorways

Manufacture: ceramics, charcoal, bricks, wire drawing, lead, steel, tools, cutlery, paper, weaving (velvet, silk, linen, wool), brushes, millstones, buttons, paint, needles, nails

Extraction: coal and chert mining, quarrying and stone masonry, lead and copper mining and ore dressing

Military: trenches, camps, aircraft crashes, bomb craters

Spiritual: churches, stone circles, burial sites

Waste disposal: middens, tips, sewers, streams, drainage

Conservation and leisure activities: rock climbing, walking, fell running, burning moorland heather for shooting

Background to this book

Walking in all seasons and in all weathers has been a key influence on my life and on the writing of this book. Moving house to the edge of the city in 2004 enabled me to walk and spend time outside in urban, rural and in-between settings more easily and more often. These local walks, time spent outside gardening and latterly at our allotment, underpin the ideas, illustrations and suggestions in this book. In my new setting I noticed that although I visited and walked many of the same places and paths, my experience was different every time. Perhaps the light was duller or brighter, the season warmer or cooler, the time of day was different. The extremes of high summer and deep winter caught my attention first. Here, on the very southern edge of the Pennines, the contrast between the summer and winter solstices at the opposite ends of the year is wide. I began to look more closely at each season as it passed and noticed the subtle changes that build up to move the year forwards. During extreme winters I was able to observe my locality transformed by ice and snow. I kept on walking, taking photos, observing and making notes about what I had seen and experienced.

I gradually gave up the childhood idea that the year has four seasons with clear beginnings and distinct endings. I began to notice that it was all much more subtle; tiny changes that accumulated day by day and eventually a new season had fully begun.

I have taken photographs for many years, documenting my walks and travels. The arrival of digital photography, especially the mobile-phone camera, has enabled me to use photography much more in my life and creative processes. The speed and immediacy of digital photography, its low cost and the ready availability of a camera at almost all times as part of my mobile phone have been transformational for me, my creative processes and my textile art.

This book reflects many aspects of my life: a rural childhood, my work as a quilter and textile artist, my education in geography, geology and archaeology and embroidery, as well as my current location. For many years my stitched textile work drew on traditional North Country quilting ideas and techniques. If you are interested in learning more about traditional North Country quilting have a look at the bibliography. If you are interested in finding out more about my earlier textile work please see my previous book *Mark-making in Textile Art* and my website.

Acknowledgements

The support and encouragement of friends, colleagues and students in all areas of life is essential. I appreciatively acknowledge all those people who have shared in and contributed to my life and creative journey thus far. Particular thanks in the making of this book to Victoria for her encouragement and proofreading, and to my beloved husband Malcolm Warrington without whom this book would simply not have happened.

Index

Picture credits

Helen Parrott
Pages 4, 5 (except top centre left and bottom right), 6, 8, 10, 13, 15, 21, 22 (except bottom left), 23, 24 (top left), 29, 34, 38, 39, 46, 47, 54, 59 (left), 65, 72, 75, 76 (left centre), 81, 82/83 (top centre), 86, 88, 90, 92/93, 96 (lower two images), 100, 103 (left), 107, 108, 109, 110–111, 112–113, 118.

Michael Wicks
Pages: 2, 3, 5 (top left), 34, 16, 22 (bottom left), 24-27, 30-33, 35, 36/37, 40-45, 50-53, 56, 57, 59 (right), 60, 61, 62, 63 (except far right), 64, 66/67, 68-71, 76 (except centre left), 77, 79, 82, 83 (except top centre), 84-85, 87, 95, 96 (upper images), 97, 98-99, 102, 103 (right), 104–106, 112/113, 120–123, 127.

Dick Makin
Pages 5: (bottom right), 18, 63 (right), 78, 114–115 (bottom of page).

Bradford Textile Archive, Bradford College
Pages: 114–115 (top two images).

Susan Denton
Page 48.